CAEL VOCABULARY PREPARATION BOOK: ACADEMIC VOCABULARY IMPROVEMENT FOR THE CAEL TEST

NOTE: Paragon Testing Enterprises, a subsidiary of The University of British Columbia, has acquired CAEL from Carleton University. This publication is not affiliated with or endorsed by Paragon Testing Services, the University of British Columbia, or Carleton University.

HOW TO USE THIS PUBLICATION:

This publication contains vocabulary like you will see on the CAEL examination.

The vocabulary in the book is divided into alphabetized sections, from A to Z. You should study the vocabulary in each section, paying special attention to how the words are used in the example sentences provided. You should also devote some time to studying the derivative words for each item. For optimal performance on the exam, it is advisable to try to commit the words to memory.

Once you have studied each section, you should proceed to the exercises at the end of the chapter. The exercises will provide you with further practice in utilizing the vocabulary naturally in sentences, a skill which is assessed on the exam.

You should then check your answers to the exercises by looking at the answer key provided at the end of the book.

ABBREVIATIONS USED IN THIS PUBLICATION:

adj.	adjective
adv.	adverb
ant.	antonym
der.	derivative
e.g.	example
esp.	especially
exp.	expression
id.	idiom
met.	metaphorical
n.	noun
p. part.	past part ciple
ph. v.	phrasal verb
sbdy	somebody
sthg	something
syn.	synonym
v.	verb

TABLE OF CONTENTS

Words – A

Instructions: Study the words below, paying attention to their meanings as well as how they are used in the example sentences. Then complete the exercise that follows.

abashed - (adj.) embarrassed. e.g. - She is easily <u>abashed</u> and often turns red from embarrassment. Der. (v.) abash; (adj.) bashful.

abdomen - (n.) the part of the body between the chest and legs. e.g. - The pregnant woman's <u>abdomen</u> grew larger every month. Der. (adj.) abdominal.

abscond - (v.) to leave a place secretly and go into hiding with stolen money. e.g. - Jeff stole money from the company for which he was chief accountant. Later, he <u>absconded</u> with the funds and is currently thought to be living in Brazil.

absorb - (v.) to use up or totally command someone's attention. e.g. - He is <u>absorbed</u> in his studies at present and rarely has time for anything else. Der. (n.) absorbency; (adj.) absorbent.

abstemious - (adj.) refraining from indulgence in food or drink. e.g. - An <u>abstemious</u> lifestyle is required in order to lose weight. Der. (adv.) abstemiously.

abstinence - (n.) the action of refraining from or not participating in certain activities. <u>Abstinence</u> from smoking will ensure good health. Der. (v.) abstain.

accessible - (adj.) being readily available or unrestricted. e.g. - Many buildings are not <u>accessible</u> to people in wheelchairs. Der. (n.) access; (n.) accessibility; (v.) access.

accommodation - (n.) the provision of rooms or housing. e.g. - The <u>accommodation</u> in the hotel was not as advertised since the rooms didn't have air conditioning. Der. (v.) accommodate.

accompany - (v.) to go along with; (syn.) escort. e.g. - I will <u>accompany</u> you to dinner. I will pick you up at your house at 6:00. Der. (n.) accompaniment.

accost - (v.) to attack; to confront aggressively. e.g. - He was <u>accosted</u> by an attacker in the street and was badly injured.

accumulate - (v.) to increase gradually in amount or quantity. e.g. - She did not become a millionaire overnight. She accumulated her wealth over many years. Der. (n.) accumulation; (adj.) accumulative; (adv.) accumulatively.

accustomed (to) - (adj.) having become familiar with or used to certain conditions because of habit or experience. e.g. - I became <u>accustomed</u> to getting up early after having had a class at 8:00 this term. Der. (v.) accustom.

acquit - (v.) to find an accused suspect not guilty of a crime in court. e.g. - The suspect was <u>acquitted</u> of the crime when he was found "not guilty" by the court. Der. (n.) acquittal.

acute - (adj.) sharp; in very serious condition. e.g. - She had an <u>acute</u> pain in her stomach and was rushed to the hospital.

1

adage - (n.) an expression, saying, or proverb. e.g. - My favourite <u>adage</u> is: Don't count your chickens before they are hatched.

adaptable - (adj.) easily accepting change. e.g. - This product is <u>adaptable</u>. It has 1001 different uses. Der. (n.) adaptability (v.) adapt.

adhesive - (adj.) self-sticking. e.g. - This label is <u>adhesive</u>. Remove the paper from the back of it and stick it on your notebook. Der. (n.) adhesiveness; (v.) adhere; (adv.) adhesively.

adjacent - (adj.) being next door or nearby. e.g. - You don't need to go far to buy bread. There is a grocery store <u>adjacent</u> to our house. Der. (n.) adjacency.

adjourn - (v.) to dismiss a meeting or call it to a close. e.g. - The business meeting began at 12:00 and was <u>adjourned</u> at 2:00.

adornment - (n.) decoration or beautification. e.g. - Her wedding dress was decorated with many <u>adornments</u>. Der. (v.) adorn.

advent (of) - (n.) arrival; coming into use or existence. e.g. - The <u>advent</u> of the new computer system means that the old system will be disposed of.

adversary - (n.) enemy, opponent, or antagonist. e.g. - The boxer hit his <u>adversary</u> with great strength. Der. (n.) adversity; (adj.) adversarial.

adverse - (adj.) negative or in opposition to the interests of. e.g. - <u>Adverse</u> weather conditions made travel out of the question. Der. (n.) adversity; (adv.) adversely.

advocate - (n.) defender or supporter of a specific cause or issue; (syn.) proponent. e.g. - He is an <u>advocate</u> of that political party since he supports their policies. Der. (v.) advocate.

affable - (adj.) pleasant; friendly; (syn.) winsome, amiable, cordial. e.g. - James is an <u>affable</u> fellow and is pleasant company. Der. (n.) affability; (adv.) affably.

affiliation - (n.) an association or close relationship of members of a group; (syn.) alliance. e.g. - Many large companies are actually an <u>affiliation</u> of several smaller companies. Der. (v.) affiliate.

affirm - (v.) to promise or declare positively. e.g. - I <u>affirm</u> that I will provide my assistance in the matter. You can depend on me. Der. (n.) affirmation.

afflict (with) - (v.) to cause pain or suffering. e.g. - She has been <u>afflicted</u> with cancer and is currently undergoing therapy. Der. (n.) affliction.

affluent - (adj.) rich; wealthy; well-to-do; well-off. e.g. - Alan is from an <u>affluent</u> family. They own five cars, three houses, and a yacht. Der. (n.) affluence; (adv.) affluently.

agrarian - (adj.) relating to farming or agriculture. e.g. - <u>Agrarian</u> businesses include the production of crops, as well as raising animals for resale.

ailment - (n.) an illness or disease. e.g. - He is suffering from a strange <u>ailment</u> and has been in bed for three weeks. Der. (v.) ail; (adj.) ailing.

alacrity - (n.) the willingness or readiness to carry out a specific action. e.g. - Sarah is an eager student and studies with <u>alacrity</u>.

alibi - (n.) an excuse used to free oneself from blame. e.g. - The suspect's <u>alibi</u> for the crime was that he was out of town when the murder took place.

alignment - (n.) the process of balancing or putting into line. e.g. - The desks in the classroom were in perfect <u>alignment</u>, with one exactly in front of the other. Der. (v.) align.

alliance - (n.) co-operation of allies or members; (syn.) affiliation. e.g. - The United Kingdom and the United States often form <u>alliances</u>, especially during times of war. Der. (adj.) allied.

allocate - (v.) to set aside in shares. e.g. - The profit was evenly <u>allocated</u> among all the partners of the company. Der. (n.) allocation; (adj.) allocated.

allot - (v.) to allocate or distribute in shares. e.g. - The father had a dozen cookies and <u>allotted</u> four of them to each of his three children. Der. (n.) allotment; (adj.) allotted.

allude (to)- (v.) to imply by inference or indirect speech. e.g. - He <u>alluded</u> to the idea that I had become fat by asking if I was wearing a larger dress size now. Der. (n.) allusion.

aloof - (adj.) arrogant; conceited. (syn.) stuck-up. e.g. - Bryce is so <u>aloof</u> that he often avoids our company. He feels that we aren't good enough for him. Der. (n.) aloofness; (adv.) aloofly.

altruistic - (adj.) relating to concern for the well-being of others. e.g. - He is one of the most <u>altruistic</u> men in the city as he constantly gives money to the poor. Der. (n.) altruism.

ambiance - (n.) atmosphere; surroundings. e.g. - The <u>ambiance</u> at the party was very cheerful. Everyone was in a great mood.

ambiguous - (adj.) unclear in meaning. e.g. - The professor's instructions were so <u>ambiguous</u> that none of the students could understand them. Der. (n.) ambiguity; (adv.) ambiguously.

ambush - (v.) to attack unexpectedly after lying in wait, esp. in battle. e.g. - The army was <u>ambushed</u> by their enemies, who had been hiding in a nearby forest. Der. (n.) ambush.

amiable - (adj.) pleasant; friendly; (syn.) affable, winsome, cordial. e.g. - Pam has an <u>amiable</u> personality and makes friends easily. Der. (adv.) amiably.

amiss - (adv.) wrong; mistaken. e.g. - I hope you won't take it <u>amiss</u> if I ask whether you have gained weight.

ancestor - (n.) a person born in a previous generation. e.g. - My <u>ancestors</u> left Europe to come to America 150 years ago.

animosity - (n.) feelings of hostility which can result in aggression. e.g. - Bob felt great <u>animosity</u> towards his boss for being unfairly fired.

3

antecedent - (adj.) relating to a preceding or previous event or circumstance. e.g. - A series of negotiations were <u>antecedent</u> to reaching a final agreement. Der. (n.) antecedent.

appalling - (adj.) causing shock or disbelief; (syn.) atrocious. e.g. - John's performance on the exam was <u>appalling</u>. Der. (v.) appal.

apparel - (n.) clothing; garments. e.g. - The department store sells all kinds of clothing, including men's, women's, and children's <u>apparel</u>.

apparent - (adj.) not hidden; open to sight; obvious; (syn.) evident. e.g. - It is <u>apparent</u> from your red nose that you have a cold. Der. (adv.) apparently.

appease - (v.) to calm or subdue. e.g. - We bought the whining children ice cream in an attempt to <u>appease</u> them. Der. (n.) appeasement; (adj.) appeasing.

appellation - (n.) a name or title. e.g. - Her <u>appellation</u> was the Queen of Sheba.

appliance - (n.) a piece of machinery or equipment used for a specific purpose, usually in the home or office. e.g. - The washing machine is such a useful appliance.

apply oneself – (id.) to work very hard on a specific task. e.g. - If we <u>apply ourselves</u>, we should be able to clean up the house in two hours.

apposite - (adj.) appropriate or suitable under the circumstances. e.g. - Louise is in the hospital, so I think that sending her some flowers would <u>apposite</u>. Der. (adv.) appositely.

apprehend - (v.) to capture a criminal who has escaped from the law. e.g. - The prisoner escaped while being transported, but was <u>apprehended</u> three days later. Der. (n.) apprehension; (adj.) apprehensible.

apprehension - (n.) fear caused by uncertainty. e.g.- Sally has a lot of <u>apprehension</u> about starting her new job. She's a nervous wreck. Der. (v.) apprehend; (adj.) apprehensive.

arduous - (adj.) exceptionally difficult or demanding. e.g. - The expedition to the North Pole was <u>arduous</u> and left the explorers exhausted. Der. (adv.) arduously.

as hard as nails – (id.) relating to a person who is strong and determined. e.g. - He won't give up. He's <u>as hard as nails</u>.

avid - (adj.) eager; enthusiastic. e.g. - He is an <u>avid</u> reader and reads three books a week. Der. (n.) avidity, avidness; (adv.) avidly.

Exercises – A

Instructions: Complete the sentences below, using one of the words beginning with the letter "A" from the previous section. Note that some gaps require a single word, while others may need a phrasal verb or idiomatic expression. You may also need to change the form of the word. The answers are provided at the end of book.

1) The _____ of the hospital with the health insurance company was an astute business venture.

2) He will _____ me to the movie, so I won't have to go alone.

3) There was a great deal of _____ between the two families because of a long-standing dispute.

4) The final exam is going to be _____, so you had better be well prepared.

5) That road will not be _____ because of the recent snowstorm.

6) This _____ can be used stick pieces of wood together.

7) The two teams were _____, and there was a great deal of rivalry between them.

8) The suspect had an _____ for the bank robbery since he was out of town at the time of the crime.

9) She _____ that I may have been lying by saying that my story was difficult to believe.

10) The _____ at the restaurant was so romantic with its candlelight and music.

Words – B

Instructions: Study the words below, paying attention to their meanings as well as how they are used in the example sentences. Then complete the exercise that follows.

babble - (v.) to talk quickly or incoherently. e.g. - Roseanne was <u>babbling</u> so fast about the accident that no one could understand her. Der. (n.) babble.

backing - (n.) the open expression of approval or support; endorsement. e.g. - She received the enthusiastic <u>backing</u> of her parents when she announced that she would marry the millionaire. Der. (v.) back.

baffle - (v.) to confuse or stupefy. e.g. - I can't understand this math homework. It completely <u>baffles</u> me.

banish - (v.) to drive out or force to leave. e.g. - You are <u>banished</u> from this club forever. Don't even try to come back here again. Der. (n.) banishment.

banner - (n.) a large piece of cloth bearing a message or national symbol; (syn.) ensign. e.g. - The fans displayed a message on a <u>banner</u> encouraging their team.

bargain - (n.) a sale or purchase at an advantageous price. e.g. - The motorcycle was a <u>bargain</u>. The original price was £1,000, and he paid only £200. Der. (v.) bargain.

barge in - (ph. v.) to enter unannounced. She always <u>barges in</u> without knocking.

barrier - (n.) something that inhibits or prevents progress or movement; (syn.) stumbling block, hindrance, obstacle. e.g. - A <u>barrier</u> was placed at the end of the street to prevent cars from entering.

bashful - (adj.) shy or self-conscious. e.g. - Mary is so <u>bashful</u> that she often finds it difficult to make new friends. Der. (v.) abash.

battle - (n.) a fight between two opposing armies; (syn.) combat. e.g. - Many soldiers died from gunshot wounds inflicted in the <u>battle</u>. Der. (v.) battle.

be a basket case - (id.) to be in very bad physical or mental condition, esp. from nervousness or exhaustion. e.g. - Mary is a <u>basket case</u> about her exams.

be caught red-handed - (id.) to be discovered during the commission of criminal activities. e.g. - He was <u>caught red-handed</u> as he attempted to put the stolen merchandise in his pocket.

be in ruins - (id.) to be totally destroyed. e.g. - The town was <u>in ruins</u> after the storm.

be of strong moral fibre - (id.) to be of good moral character. e.g. - Dylan would never lie or steal. He is <u>of strong moral fibre</u>.

beating about the bush - (id.) to avoid talking about a certain topic. e.g. - I tried to get an answer out of her, but she kept on <u>beating about the bush</u>.

beckon - (v.) to call forward. e.g. - The teacher is <u>beckoning</u> you to come forward to the board.

belittle - (v.) to cause to feel inferior. e.g. - Sam always <u>belittles</u> his wife by telling her how stupid she is. Actually, she is quite intelligent.

bequest - (n.) the action of leaving money or specific property to another person upon an individual's death. e.g. - A <u>bequest</u> in my uncle's will specifically states that I shall receive £10,000 when he dies. Der. (v.) bequeath.

beseech - (v.) to beg; (syn.) implore; entreat; (p. part.) besought. e.g. - The victim <u>besought</u> the attacker not to kill him.

beset - (v.) to cause trouble or difficulties. e.g. - Tina has been <u>beset</u> with difficulties all her life.

beside yourself – (id.) to be very nervous or upset. e.g. - I am just <u>beside myself</u> waiting for the results of my test.

beverage - (n.) any alcoholic or non-alcoholic drink. e.g. - I was thirsty and wanted to drink a cold <u>beverage</u>.

beyond my wildest dreams - (id.) to be better than your highest expectations. e.g. - My vacation in Rome was <u>beyond my wildest dreams</u>.

biased - (adj.) relating to prejudice caused by an unfair or irrational belief or preference. e.g. - A judge must never be <u>biased</u>, but must treat all people fairly and equally. Der. (n.) bias; (v.) bias.

bigoted - (adj.) relating to prejudice because of race, colour, or national origin. e.g. - He is so <u>bigoted</u>. He always says negative and inappropriate things about people of other races. Der. (n.) bigot.

bland - (adj.) tasteless or lacking in flavour; (syn.) insipid. e.g. - These potatoes are <u>bland</u>. I think they could use some salt. Der. (n.) blandness; (adv.) blandly.

blandishment - (n.) compliment. e.g. - Mike gave me a nice <u>blandishment</u> yesterday. He told me that I was the most beautiful girl he'd ever seen. Der. (v.) blandish.

bleak - (adj.) hopeless; depressing. e.g. - What <u>bleak</u> weather! Grey sky and rain get me down. Der. (n.) bleakness; (adv.) bleakly.

blister - (n.) a raised area of skin which contains water or fluid. e.g. - These shoes are too small. They have given me <u>blisters</u> on my feet.

blow - (n.) the action of striking or hitting. e.g. - The boxer fell to the floor when struck by his opponent's <u>blow</u>.

blow your chances - (id.) to lose all opportunities for success in an activity. e.g. - He <u>blew his chances</u> of buying a car by losing all his money gambling.

blue - (id.) relating to extreme sadness or depression. e.g. - Julie felt <u>blue</u> after her boyfriend left her. I've never seen her so down.

bluff - (n.) the steep side of a mountain; cliff. e.g. - An excellent view of the city can be seen when looking down from the nearby bluff.

失误 **blunder** - (n.) error; mistake. e.g. - The accident resulted from his blunder in failing to signal his turn.

毛钝 **blunt** - (adj.) not sharp; dull. e.g. - The victim was struck with a blunt object, such as a flat rock or brick. Der. (adv.) bluntly.

模糊的 **blurry** - (adj.) unclear or lacking in focus. e.g. - My vision is always blurry when I'm not wearing my glasses. Der. (n.) blur, blurriness; (v.) blur; (adj.) blurred; (adv.) blurrily.

脱口而出 **blurt** - (v.) to say something suddenly and unexpectedly. e.g. - He blurted out the location of the surprise party.

假的 **bogus** - (adj.) not authentic; fake; (syn.) phony. e.g. - The bogus painting of the "Mona Lisa" is often mistaken for the genuine one.

支持 **bolster** - (v.) to raise or increase by supporting the cause or interest of something. e.g. - Going to Disneyland bolstered the spirits of the terminally-ill children.

繁荣兴 **boom** - (v.) to experience great success or expansion; prosper. e.g. - The college is building 盛 new classrooms because enrolment is booming. Der. (n.) boom.

booth - (n.) an area enclosed by temporary walls on three or more sides. e.g. - He placed a telephone call from a public phone booth.

bored to tears - (id.) very bored. e.g. - The lesson was hardly interesting. In fact, I was bored to tears.

丰富 **bountiful** - (adj.) existing in great quantity or variety. e.g. - That supermarket has a bountiful selection of different types of food. Der. (n.) bounty; (adv.) bountifully.

box office - (id.) the cashier's office at a cinema. e.g. - We bought our tickets at the box office at the cinema.

争吵 **brawl** - (v.) to fight or engage in physical contact. e.g. - Three young men were brawling in the street. As a result, two were sent to the hospital. Der. (n.) brawl.

违反 **breach** - (v.) to break or violate the law. e.g. - If you park in a prohibited area, you will breach the law. Der. (n.) breach.

break down - (ph. v.) to destroy or remove. e.g. - Their relationship broke down due to their constant arguments about money.

品种 **breed** - (n.) class, kind, or type. e.g. - The zoo displayed numerous breeds of animals. Der. (v.) breed.

贿赂 **bribe** - (n.) money given to influence the judgment of a public official. e.g. - He offered money to the policeman as a bribe in order to avoid paying a heavy fine. Der. (v.) bribe.

缘 **brim** - (n.) the top edge of a cup. e.g. - That cup is filled to the <u>brim</u>. If you bump it, it will spill.

上劲 **budge** - (v.) to move sthg with difficulty. e.g. - Alan tried to move the heavy cabinet, but it wouldn't <u>budge</u>.

bump - (n.) a small, raised area. e.g. - Janice had a <u>bump</u> on her head from hitting it on the steering wheel of the car in the accident. Der. (v.) bump.

浮标 **buoy** - (n.) a floating object that indicates a dangerous area in a waterway. e.g. - Don't swim beyond the red and white <u>buoys</u> floating in the water. It's too deep to swim out there. Der. (n.) buoyancy; (adj.) buoyant; (adv.) buoyantly.

bureaucratic - (adj.) relating to the administration of the government. e.g. - I had a lot of <u>bureaucratic</u> hassle at the court house this morning when I went to re-new my driver's license. Der. (n.) bureaucracy.

埋葬 **burial** - (n.) the action of placing something under the ground, esp. the body of the deceased in a funeral. e.g. - The dog has many bad habits, the most annoying of which is the <u>burial</u> of bones in our front yard. Der. (v.) bury.

忙碌 **bustle** - (v.) to move hurriedly, esp. in order to prepare something. e.g. - Anne had to <u>bustle</u> around this morning. She overslept and was late for work.

butter sbdy up - (id.) to win someone's favour through flattery. e.g. - He tried to <u>butter me up</u> by saying how beautiful I looked today.

by leaps and bounds - (id.) with incredible or amazing speed. e.g. - The world population crisis is evident in countries such as India, where the population has grown <u>by leaps and bounds</u>.

Exercises – B

Instructions: Complete the sentences below, using one of the words beginning with the letter "B" from the previous section. Note that some gaps require a single word, while others may need a phrasal verb or idiomatic expression. You may also need to change the form of the word. The answers are provided at the end of book.

1) He wouldn't give be a straight answer, but just kept on _____.

2) She tried to _____ me up by saying how clever she thought I was.

3) You will _____ your rental agreement if you leave without paying twelve months' rent.

4) The ship entered the prohibited zone, even though there were _____ demarcating the area.

5) Their business relationship _____ because they couldn't agree on a management strategy.

6) Her food is always so _____ since she refuses to use any spice or seasoning.

7) She _____ her husband with constant insults. I don't know how he puts up with it.

8) The last section of the exam _____ me. I doubt if I got a single question correct.

9) Telling me I was beautiful and intelligent was such a nice _____.

10) I was _____ in class today. There was nothing new or interesting in the class material.

Words – C

Instructions: Study the words below, paying attention to their meanings as well as how they are used in the example sentences. Then complete the exercise that follows.

cagey - (adj.) relating to the use of cleverness and dishonesty. e.g. - The cagey criminal robbed me after visiting my home under the pretence of being an insurance salesman.

calamity - (n.) disaster; catastrophe. e.g. - The earthquake was one of country's worst natural calamities.

call for sthg - (id.) to make something necessary or required. e.g. - This recipe calls for white wine.

calling - (n.) vocation. e.g. - He felt that his calling was to be a doctor.

campaign - (n.) participation as a candidate in a political election. e.g. - He was an assistant in the political campaign. Der. (v.) campaign.

candour - (n.) honesty; frankness. e.g. - If I can speak with candour, I must tell you that your behaviour is entirely unacceptable. Der. (adj.) candid; (adv.) candidly.

capitulate - (v.) to give up or surrender in battle. e.g. - The army capitulated after the enemy's heavy attack. Der. (n.) capitulation.

capsize - (v.) to overturn a boat in a waterway. e.g. - The passenger fell overboard into the water when the boat capsized.

carcass - (n.) the body of a dead animal. e.g. - The carcass of a dead dog, which had been hit by a car, was lying in the centre of the road.

carnivorous - (adj.) relating to animals that consume meat. e.g. - Animals such as dogs are carnivorous. They do not eat grass, but rather eat meat. Der (n.) carnivore.

cask - (n.) a round wooden container used for storing alcoholic beverages; barrel. e.g. - Whisky and beer are usually stored in large casks when they are manufactured.

cast aspersions on sbdy's character - (id.) to damage someone's reputation through rumours or gossip. e.g. - I would never cast aspersions on his character. In fact, I know that he is a very nice person.

catch - (v.)(met.) to hear or to understand. e.g. - Did you catch what he just said?

cavity - (n.) a small hole in something. e.g. - If you eat too many sweets, you will get cavities in your teeth.

censure - (v.) to experience public criticism by one's colleagues. e.g. - The lawyer was censured by the committee for attempting to steal money from a client. Der. (n.) censure.

champion - (v.) to support a cause or campaign strongly. e.g. - He <u>championed</u> the abolition of the death penalty.

chant - (v.) to sing in a monotonous voice, esp. during religious worship. e.g. - It is difficult for Debbie to sing with a group since she <u>chants</u> in a monotone and finds it difficult to sing a melody

chaperon - (n.) an individual who accompanies or goes with another. e.g. - An attractive young man was her <u>chaperon</u> for the evening. Der. (v.) chaperon.

charge (with) - (v.) to accuse an individual of the commission of a crime. e.g. - The police came to the suspect's house with legal documents to <u>charge</u> her with the crime of robbery.

charming - (adj.) exceptionally pleasant, as if magical. e.g. - David is a <u>charming</u> man. He has many friends since it is so easy to enjoy his company. Der. (n.) charm; (v.) charm.

chaste - (adj.) pure or clean in character, esp. sexually. e.g. - A rapist can hardly be considered <u>chaste</u>. Der. (n.) chastity.

cheat on - (id.) to be unfaithful to one's spouse or romantic partner. e.g. - Tom is filing for divorce because his wife was <u>cheating on</u> him.

check sthg out - (id.) to look at or verify something. e.g. - <u>Check out</u> the story in this newspaper. It's really amazing.

chequered past - (id.) to have undesirable experiences in one's past. e.g. - Bob doesn't speak about his life in London. He must have a <u>chequered past</u>.

chew - (v.) to move the teeth together and apart when eating. e.g. - Food must be <u>chewed</u> well before swallowing.

chortle - (v.) to laugh. e.g. - The funny joke made us all <u>chortle</u>.

cinder - (n.) a small grey fragment which remains after a fire is extinguished. e.g. - Small <u>cinders</u> drifted in the smoke from the factory chimney.

civilian - (n.) an individual not on duty in the armed services. e.g. - Since the soldier was not on active duty in the army, he was dressed as a <u>civilian</u>.

clandestine - (adj.) being done or carried out in secrecy. e.g. - The <u>clandestine</u> government operation was known only to a select group of politicians. Der. (adv.) clandestinely.

clarify - (v.) to make clear in meaning. e.g. - The teacher explained the homework again in order to <u>clarify</u> the instructions. Der. (n.) clarity, clarification.

classify - (v.) to place into groups or categories. e.g. - The advertisements were <u>classified</u> according to employment opportunities and items offered for sale. Der. (n.) classification; (adj.) classified.

clip - (v.) to cut quickly, esp. with a scissors. He showed me an article that he had <u>clipped</u> out of a magazine.

clot - (n.) the formation of blood into a hardened lump. e.g. - It looks as though that wound will stop bleeding now. I think a <u>clot</u> is beginning to form. Der. (v.) clot; (adj.) clotted.

clutter - (n.) a disorganized collection of various items. e.g. - It took Laura two days to organize the <u>clutter</u> left on her desk while she was away from the office on holiday. Der. (adj.) cluttered.

coax - (v.) to influence, persuade, or manipulate; (syn.) cajole. e.g. - Christine was not in the mood to go to the party, but we <u>coaxed</u> her into going by saying that her boyfriend would be there.

cog - (n.) a small tooth-like piece on a wheel-shaped gear. e.g. - The clock was not working because a small <u>cog</u> on the inside had broken off.

cogent - (adj.) logical and credible. e.g. - Saying that the earth is flat is hardly a <u>cogent</u> statement. Der. (adv.) cogently.

collaboration - (n.) the action of working together with others; (syn.) cooperation. e.g. - The <u>collaboration</u> of all the factory workers made everyone's job easier. Der. (v.) collaborate.

colossal - (adj.) amazing or incredible in size. e.g. - The elephant is a <u>colossal</u> animal, often weighing several tons.

comb - (v.)(met.) to search extensively for something, esp. with difficulty. e.g. - The police are <u>combing</u> the city in search of the escaped criminal.

commemorate - (v.) to serve as a reminder for events of particular historical significance. e.g. - Remembrance Day is celebrated to <u>commemorate</u> the lives lost in former wars. Der. (n.) commemoration; (adj.) commemorative.

commence - (v.) to begin; to start. e.g. - The T.V. program <u>commenced</u> at 8:00 and finished at 9:00. Der. (n.) commencement.

commended - (adj.) deserving of special praise, notice, or attention. e.g. - The soldier was <u>commended</u> for bravery in battle by receiving a special commendation. Der. (n.) commendation; (v.) commend.

commentary - (n.) a systematic explanation of events. e.g. - He often provides <u>commentary</u> during televised football games. Der. (n.) commentator; (v.) comment.

commercial - (adj.) relating to business or finance. Banking and investments are <u>commercial</u> activities. Der. (n.) commerce; (adv.) commercially.

commodity - (n.) any item that can be bought and sold in the marketplace. e.g. - Gold and silver are precious <u>commodities</u> that are readily exchanged in the marketplace.

compassion - (n.) the state of being full of mercy. e.g. - The doctor displayed great <u>compassion</u> toward the dying man. Der. (adj.) compassionate; (adv.) compassionately.

compel - (v.) to cause or bring out through force or pressure. e.g. - His parents <u>compelled</u> him to attend college, although he didn't want to. Der. (n.) compulsion; (adj.) compelling.

component - (n.) an integral or necessary part of something. e.g. - All of the <u>components</u> must be working in order for the machine to function properly.

comprehensive - (adj.) complete; all-inclusive. e.g. - The examination is <u>comprehensive</u>. It covers the entire textbook. Der. (n.) comprehensiveness; (adv.) comprehensively.

compress - (v.) to apply with great pressure. e.g. - This machine can <u>compress</u> a large amount of garbage into one small package. Der. (n.) compress; (adj.) compressed.

compulsory - (adj.) required; necessary; obligatory; (syn.) mandatory. e.g. - Class attendance is <u>compulsory</u>. You are required to attend.

concatenation - (n.) the series of items linked in different orders. e.g. - There are many <u>concatenations</u> of human DNA. Der. (v.) concatenate.

concentrate - (n.) a product that has been reduced in size as a result of dehydration. e.g. - This new dishwashing liquid is a <u>concentrate</u>. Only one-quarter of the normal amount should be used. Der. (n.) concentration; (v.) concentrate; (adj.) concentrated.

concoction - (n.) a food or drink that has been prepared from a combination of ingredients which are often mysterious or unknown. e.g. - Marisa refused to tell us the ingredients of the <u>concoction</u> she had made, saying that the recipe was a secret. Der. (v.) concoct; (adj.) concocted.

condone - (v.) to view as unimportant; to overlook. Your behaviour is unacceptable, and I cannot <u>condone</u> it. Der. (adj.) condonable.

conducive (to) - (adj.) beneficial; helpful. e.g. - A quiet weekend in the countryside is <u>conducive</u> to relaxation. Der. (v.) conduce.

confection - (n.) any sweet or dessert; food made with sugar. e.g. - That store sells all kinds of <u>confections</u>, including chocolate, cakes, and biscuits. Der. (adj.) confectionary.

confession - (n.) the admission of guilt or wrongdoing. e.g. - After several denials, the suspect finally signed a full <u>confession</u> of the crime. Der. (v.) confess.

confidential - (adj.) secret; private; personal. e.g. - This letter is <u>confidential</u> and should be read only by the person to whom it is addressed. Der. (n.) confidence; (v.) confide; (adv.) confidentially.

confine - (v.) to cause to become limited in room or space. e.g. - The prisoner was <u>confined</u> to his cell twenty-three hours a day and often dreamed of freedom. Der. (n.) confinement; (adj.) confined.

conflagration - (n.) a great fire. e.g. - The fire department was called to put out the <u>conflagration</u>.

conform (to) - (v.) to agree to or comply with a standard. e.g. - Those individuals who do not <u>conform</u> to the rules of the club will be denied membership. Der. (n.) conformity.

congregation - (n.) a gathering of individuals. e.g. - There was a large congregation of people at the war memorial service. Der. (v.) congregate.

conjugation - (n.) the formation of pairs or groups. e.g. - Many grammatical exercises involve the conjugation of verbs. Der. (v.) conjugate.

consensus - (n.) agreement by members of a group. e.g. - After fifteen minutes of discussion, the group finally reached a consensus about what restaurant to go to.

consistency - (1)(n.) texture; firmness; (2)(n.) the quality of not changing. e.g. - (1) The consistency of the apple was too soft. We knew that it was not fit to eat. (2) Mary has shown consistency in her performance at college this year. She has received A's all semester. Der. (adj.) consistent; (adv.) consistently.

console - (v.) to soothe or comfort. e.g. - Terri was crying, so we tried to console her by saying that everything was going to be alright. Der. (n.) consolation.

consolidate - (v.) to join together; unite; merge. e.g. - The two companies consolidated to form a new, larger company. Der. (n.) consolidation; (adj.) consolidated.

conspicuous - (adj.) noticeable; capable of drawing attention. e.g. - Tim's wealth was conspicuous by the large amounts of money he spent. Der. (n.) conspicuousness; (adv.) conspicuously.

constituent - (n.) a citizen of a particular political district who is eligible to vote in elections. e.g. - The constituents of London will vote for a new mayor in the forthcoming elections. Der. (n.) constituency.

consumer - (n.) an individual who buys goods in the marketplace. e.g. - Increased purchasing by consumers has resulted in an improvement in the economy. Der. (v.) consume; (n.) consumption.

consummate - (v.) to bring to a conclusion. e.g. - The agreement was consummated when the contract was signed. Der. (n.) consummation; (adj.) consummated.

contagious - (adj.) infectious; transmitted from one individual to another. e.g. - Many childhood diseases are contagious. If one child becomes ill, other children living in the same house will also become ill. Der. (n.) contagion.

contaminate - (v.) to cause to become infected, polluted, or poisoned. e.g. - Many rivers used to be contaminated by pollution from nearby factories. Der. (n.) contamination.

contemplate - (v.) to think about or consider. e.g. - The great philosophers often contemplated the meaning of life. Der. (n.) contemplation; (adj.) contemplative; (adv.) contemplatively.

contemporary - (adj.) modern; current. e.g. - She hates old-fashioned things so her house is filled only with contemporary furniture. Der. (adv.) contemporarily.

contempt - (n.) hatred or disgust; (syn.) enmity. e.g. - Great <u>contempt</u> was shown towards the criminal by the judge, who said that the crimes shocked society. Der. (adj.) contemptible, contemptuous.

contend (with) - (v.) to deal with; to manage a difficult situation. e.g. - Police officers have to <u>contend</u> with danger and violence in their jobs. Der. (n.) contention.

contiguous - (adj.) adjoining; neighbouring; sharing a common boundary. e.g. - The northern border of the United States is <u>contiguous</u> with Canada. Der. (n.) contiguity; (adv.) contiguously.

contingent - (adj.) dependent upon unpredictable causes or events. e.g. - Our trip to the beach tomorrow is <u>contingent</u> upon the weather. Der. (n.) contingency; (adv.) contingently.

contravene - (v.) to oppose or act against the desires or wishes of another individual. e.g. - Children who <u>contravene</u> the wishes of their parents often receive punishment. Der. (n.) contravention.

contrition - (n.) the feeling of deep sorrow or regret about one's wrongdoings; (syn.) remorse, penitence. e.g. - The criminal felt great <u>contrition</u> for his crimes and was filled with regret. Der. (adj.) contrite.

contrive - (v.) to devise or plan, esp. in artistic form. e.g. - After months of planning, the prisoners finally <u>contrived</u> a way to escape. Der. (adj.) contrived.

controversial - (adj.) relating to discussion in or disagreement among the public with respect to a specific topic. e.g. - Capital punishment and abortion are highly <u>controversial</u> topics.

convalesce - (v.) to recover health after an extended illness or operation; (syn.) recuperate. e.g. - Samantha is at home <u>convalescing</u> after having surgery on her back. Der. (n.) convalescence; (adj.) convalescent.

convict (of) - (v.) to send a criminal to prison for his crime. e.g. - Michael is serving life in prison as a result of being <u>convicted</u> of murder. Der. (n.) convict, conviction; (adj.) convicted.

convivial - (adj.) cheerful; friendly. e.g. - He has a <u>convivial</u> personality and is very outgoing. Der. (n.) conviviality; (adv.) convivially.

cooperation - (n.) the action of working together with others; (syn.) collaboration. e.g. - The <u>cooperation</u> of three cardiology specialists was needed to diagnose the patient's heart condition. Der. (v.) cooperate; (adj.) cooperative; (adv.) cooperatively.

coordinate - (v.) to act or work together. e.g. - The work of several departments of the company was <u>coordinated</u> in order to make operations more efficient. Der. (n.) coordinator; (n.) coordination; (adj.) coordinated.

cordial - (adj.) friendly; (syn.) affable, amiable, winsome. e.g. - She is quite <u>cordial</u> and makes friends easily. Der. (adv.) cordially.

core - (adj.) relating to the basic or central part. e.g. The core courses must be taken during a student's first year at this college. After that, the students may choose from more specialized courses.

cork - (n.) a porous substance that is commonly used to seal the tops of bottles of wine. e.g. - A special opener is needed to remove the cork from the top of a wine bottle.

count me in - (id.) to want to participate in an activity. e.g. - I'll come to the party with you. Count me in.

counterfeit - (n.) false copies of paper money. e.g. - This money is counterfeit. It is not authentic and is, therefore, worthless. Der. (v.) counterfeit; (adj.) counterfeit.

coup - (n.) a revolutionary group that seeks to overthrow an existing government, esp. with the use of violence. e.g. - The Parliament building was seized during the coup as the rebels attempted to take control of the government.

covert - (adj.) hidden or secretive. e.g. - The details of the covert military operation were known only to the president and a few of his close assistants. Der. (n.) covertness; (adv.) covertly; (ant.) overt.

cover-up - (n.) the action of hiding despicable or blameworthy actions or events. e.g. - The cover-up of the crime involved the destruction of key evidence. Der. (ph. v.) cover up.

coy - (adj.) flirtatious or coquettish. e.g. - The woman was very coy in gaining the affection of the man. Der. (adv.) coyly.

crack sbdy up - (id.) to amuse someone. e.g. - Juan's funny jokes really crack me up.

crate - (n.) a wooden box-like container. e.g. - The oranges were transported to the grocery store in a wooden crate.

creep - (n.) an obnoxious or unpleasant person. e.g. - Don't go out with him. He's really a creep.

crevice - (n.) a narrow crack. e.g. - Barbara fell down when her heel got caught in a crevice in the sidewalk.

crimson - (adj.) dark red. e.g. - Blood is crimson in colour.

crushed - (id.) to be very disappointed. e.g. - She was crushed when her boyfriend left her.

culminate (in) - (v.) to bring to a conclusion. e.g. - The graduation ceremony culminates in the distribution of diplomas to the class. Der. (n.) culmination.

cultivation - (n.) the process of preparing the land for planting. e.g. - Cultivation begins in the spring when the top soil is turned over in order to prepare the ground for seeds or plants. Der. (v.) cultivate; (adj.) cultivated.

cumbersome - (adj.) troublesome; difficult; heavy. e.g. - Jennifer's journey was cumbersome since she carried two huge suitcases with her. Der. (v.) encumber

cumulative - (adj.) the total sum of separate parts. e.g. - The <u>cumulative</u> sum of 20 and 20 is 40. Der. (v.) cumulate; (adv.) cumulatively.

cunning - (adj.) relating to the use of dishonesty and manipulation to achieve one's ambitions; sly; (syn.) sneaky. e.g. - Jeff doesn't really love Debra. He's just being <u>cunning</u> in order to get what he wants from her. Der. (n.) cunning; (adv.) cunningly.

custody - (n.) control or guardianship over a person by an individual in authority. e.g. - Anne was granted <u>custody</u> of the children in the divorce. They now live with her. Der. (adj.) custodial.

cut off your nose to spite your face - (id.) to hurt oneself by seeking revenge on others. e.g. - I know that you don't like your teacher, but telling her that she's stupid was <u>cutting off your nose to spite your face</u>.

Exercises – C

Instructions: Complete the sentences below, using one of the words beginning with the letter "C" from the previous section. Note that some gaps require a single word, while others may need a phrasal verb or idiomatic expression. You may also need to change the form of the word. The answers are provided at the end of book.

1) We _____ when he told the funny joke.

2) The boat _____, and the passengers fell into the sea

3) There was a secret _____ in the wall where he had hidden a gun.

4) I had so much _____ in the house that my roommate told me to get organized.

5) They had a _____ relationship and had to meet in secret places.

6) The _____ of the members of staff will ensure that the project is completed more quickly.

7) The college _____ its English courses into three categories: beginner, intermediate, and advanced.

8) After weeks of refusing my request, my boss finally _____ and said I could take my vacation when I wanted.

9) That little village is so _____ with its cottages and cobblestone streets.

10) She couldn't put forward a _____ argument for her point of view, so we weren't convinced that her idea was a good one.

Words – D

Instructions: Study the words below, paying attention to their meanings as well as how they are used in the example sentences. Then complete the exercise that follows.

damp - (adj.) slightly wet or moist. e.g. - His forehead was <u>damp</u> because he had been sweating. He wiped it dry with a handkerchief. Der. (n.) damp; (v.) dampen.

dapper - (adj.) very well dressed. e.g. - He looked <u>dapper</u> in his new suit.

dash - (n.) a small portion of something added to something else. e.g. - A <u>dash</u> of salt should be added to the food.

debris - (n.) the remaining broken pieces of something. e.g. - There was a lot of <u>debris</u> on the road after the accident, including fragments of broken glass and pieces of metal.

deceased - (adj.) relating to a person who has died. e.g. - My father is <u>deceased</u>. He died ten years ago. Der. (n.) decedent.

deciduous - (adj.) relating to trees which lose their leaves seasonally. e.g. - <u>Deciduous</u> trees in Vermont turn to beautiful shades of red, orange, and yellow before losing their leaves every fall.

decorous - (adj.) correct in behaviour; in good taste. e.g. - The fireman behaved in a most <u>decorous</u> way during the blaze and cannot be blamed for the deaths that occurred. Der. (n.) decorum; (adv.) decorously.

defect - (n.) a lack of proper function which prevents use of a machine. e.g. - The stereo had a <u>defect</u> in its sound system and would not play the CD properly. Der. (adj.) defective; (adv.) defectively.

defile - (v.) to cause to become unclean or unchaste. e.g. - The environment is being <u>defiled</u> with all types of pollution and litter. Der. (n.) defilement; (adj.) defiled.

deft - (adj.) possessing great skill or ability. e.g. - Paula is quite <u>deft</u> at knitting. She made this sweater in only twelve hours. Der. (adv.) deftly.

defunct - (adj.) no longer existing or operating; no longer active. e.g. - Due to a lack of interest by its members, the club is now <u>defunct</u>.

defy - (v.) to accomplish something that is considered impossible or improper. e.g. - He <u>defied</u> his parents by getting married when he was only sixteen, although they had forbidden it. Der. (n.) defiance; (adj.) defiant; (adv.) defiantly.

deliberation - (n.) careful consideration of a topic, including reasons for and against. e.g. - After careful <u>deliberation</u> of all the advantages and disadvantages, she finally decided to attend college. Der. (v.) deliberate; (adj.) deliberate.

deluge - (n.) a sudden downpour of rain or water. e.g. - A sudden <u>deluge</u> of rain caused flooding in the city. Der. (v.) deluge.

demeanour - (n.) behaviour, manner, or temperament. e.g. - This job requires a person with a pleasant demeanour because you will constantly be working with the public.

demented - (adj.) crazy; insane. e.g. - Why are you acting so demented? Have you gone crazy or something? Der. (n.) dementedness; (adv.) dementedly.

demise - (n.) destruction or downfall. e.g. - Excessive gambling led to his demise. He lost all of his possessions as a result of his uncontrollable habit.

demoralize - (v.) to discourage; to weaken the spirit of. e.g. - Carmen was demoralized when she failed her driving test the fourth time.

denial - (n.) statement that an accusation is false. e.g. - The Prime Minister issued a full denial of any involvement in the scandal, saying that any rumours were untrue. Der. (v.) deny.

denomination - (n.) size of a value of paper money. e.g. - The bank robbers stole $10,000 in $100 and $50 denominations. Der. (v.) denominate.

denounce - (v.) to show to be false, wrong, or evil. e.g. - He denounced smoking, saying that it was a disgusting and dangerous habit. Der. (n.) denouncement.

dense - (adj.) thick or heavy. e.g. - A dense snowfall caused the highway department to close all the roads. Der. (adv.) densely.

depict - (v.) to show in the form of a picture or photograph. This photograph depicts my mother when she was a child. Der. (n.) depiction.

deplore - (v.) to consider as deserving of contempt or disapproval. e.g. - The teacher deplored the students who hadn't done their homework and expressed her disapproval. Der. (adj.) deplorable; (adv.) deplorably.

deposit - (v.) to place money in a bank account. e.g. - I am trying to save money by depositing $200 into my bank account every month. Der. (n.) deposit.

deranged - (adj.) mentally disturbed; insane; crazy. e.g. - Deranged individuals, such as psychopaths or sociopaths, are in need of psychological treatment. Der. (v.) derange.

desolate - (adj.) filled with sorrow or despair as a result of loneliness; (syn.) forlorn. e.g. - Thomas felt desolate when he moved to Manchester. He didn't have any friends and was often lonely. Der. (n.) desolation; (adj.) desolating.

despair - (v.) to feel hopelessness or extreme disappointment; (syn.) despondency. e.g. - The businessman despaired that he would never be successful when his second business failed. Der. (n.) despair.

desperation - (n.) hopelessness; despair. e.g. - The poor woman hadn't eaten in days and, in desperation, she stole food from the supermarket. Der. (adj.) desperate; (adv.) desperately.

despicable - (adj.) deserving of hate; (syn.) odious. e.g. - The crimes that he committed are despicable, and he has many enemies. Der. (adv.) despicably.

despondency - (n.) despair; depression. e.g. - In his <u>despondency</u>, he contemplated whether his life had meaning. Der. (adj.) despondent. Der. (adv.) despondently.

destine - (v.) to determine the outcome of something in advance, esp. by fate. e.g. - He is a very smart boy and is <u>destined</u> to have a bright future. Der. (n.) destiny; (adj.) destined.

detention - (n.) the process of delaying or holding back, esp. for questioning or punishment. e.g. - He was held in <u>detention</u> after school as punishment for failing to do his homework. Der. (v.) detain.

deterrent - (n.) the prevention or discouragement of illegal or improper behaviour. e.g. - The death penalty is considered to be a <u>deterrent</u> to the commission of the crime of murder, although statistics show that the murder rate increases every year. Der. (v.) deter.

detract (from) - (v.) to make less in terms of value or importance. e.g. - The crack in the vase <u>detracted</u> from its value.

devoted - (adj.) strongly committed to a purpose or cause. e.g. - He is a <u>devoted</u> doctor and often works without pay. Der. (n.) devotion; (v.) devote.

devour - (v.) to eat or use up in great quantity. e.g. - The hungry dog <u>devoured</u> its food.

dig up - (id.) to discover as a result of searching extensively. e.g. - Joe searched through his closet, trying to <u>dig up</u> something to wear.

diligent - (adj.) relating to the exercise of caution and determination. e.g. - You must be <u>diligent</u> when driving on interstate highways in order to avoid accidents. Der. (n.) diligence; (adv.) diligently.

dilute - (v.) to add water to a mixture. e.g. - The orange juice concentrate should be <u>diluted</u> and mixed before serving.

dingy - (adj.) dirty; unclean. e.g. - The hotel was so <u>dingy</u> that it looked like it hadn't been cleaned in months.

disclose - (v.) to uncover or cause to become known. e.g. - The bank robber finally <u>disclosed</u> the location of the hidden money after undergoing extensive questioning. Der. (n.) disclosure.

disconcerted - (adj.) very discouraged; disillusioned. e.g. - My cousin was <u>disconcerted</u> when he realised that his new job wasn't what he wanted after all. Der. (v.) disconcert.

discontented - (adj.) unhappy; displeased. e.g. - Many students become <u>discontented</u> with college and decide to drop out. Der (n.) discontentment, discontent.

discrepancy - (n.) disagreement or inconsistency between or among various things. e.g. - There was a <u>discrepancy</u> between the two different versions of the story. Der. (adj.) discrepant; (adv.) discrepantly.

disjointed - (adj.) lacking in sequence, order, or organization. e.g. - The professor's explanation was totally <u>disjointed</u>. As a result, none of the students understood him. Der. (v.) disjoint.

dismal - (adj.) being of particularly bad quality; disastrous; (syn.) wretched. e.g. - The weather is so dismal today with all this sleet and rain. Der. (adv.) dismally.

dismantle - (v.) to take a machine apart into pieces; disassemble. e.g. - She dismantled her furniture before moving into her new house since the individual pieces of wood would be easier to carry.

disparity - (n.) disagreement; (syn.) incongruity. e.g. - There seems to be some disparity between the story he told and the facts.

dispatch - (v.) to send, esp. quickly. e.g. - The letter was dispatched to you by courier on Thursday. Der. (n.) dispatch.

dispense - (v.) to give out in shares or measured parts. e.g. - My parents always dispense advice without me asking for it.

disposition - (n.) mood or character. e.g. - His disposition was great today. I have never seen him so cheerful. Der. (v.) dispose.

dissension - (n.) disagreement; conflict; controversy. e.g. - There is some dissension about what happened. Everyone seems to have a different version of the events. Der. (v.) dissent.

dissolute - (adj.) indulgent. e.g. - If you have dissolute eating habits, you will become fat. Der. (n.) dissolution; (adv.) dissolutely.

divergence - (n.) separation; movement apart; disunion. e.g. - Their divergence in personal opinions causes many arguments. Der. (v.) diverge; (adj.) divergent.

diversification - (n.) the action of providing variety. e.g. - This university has a great diversification of subjects, with programs ranging from animal science to marketing. Der. (v.) diversify; (adj.) diversified.

diversion - (n.) a change of course in direction or activity. e.g. - There is a traffic diversion in the center of town because the road is being repaired. Der. (v.) divert; (adj.) diverted.

domain - (n.) territory. e.g. - Don't enter this room. It is my private domain.

domestic - (adj.) relating to or coming from a specific country. e.g. - Many domestic wines are produced in Spain. Der. (n.) domesticity; (v.) domesticate; (adj.) domesticated.

domineering - (adj.) controlling or influencing excessively. e.g. - She is a domineering woman and is always telling her husband what to do. Der. (n.) domination; (v.) domineer; (adv.) domineeringly.

downfall - (n.) a situation which results in a catastrophe. e.g. - His downfall came from gambling. In fact, he lost the family fortune.

dregs - (n.) a substance that remains after a liquid has been removed from a container. e.g. - He poured the beer into a glass, leaving only the dregs at the bottom of the bottle.

drench - (v.) to become full or covered with water or moisture; (syn.) soak. e.g. - Marco got <u>drenched</u> when he was caught in the rain without an umbrella. Der. (adj.) drenched.

drive - (n.) motivation or impulse. e.g. - John is one of the laziest people I know. He has absolutely no <u>drive</u>. Der. (v.) drive; (adj.) driven.

drive a hard bargain - (id.) to be difficult to negotiate with. e.g. - He's not going to change his mind. He <u>drives a hard bargain</u>.

drop a hint - (id.) to give someone subtle ideas about something in order to express one's likes or dislikes. e.g. - He <u>dropped a hint</u> that he would like a new tie for his birthday.

drop in - (id.) to visit someone's home without having arranged a specific time. e.g. - <u>Drop in</u> and see me sometime!

dubious - (adj.) doubtful in quality. e.g. - He told us a <u>dubious</u> story about a series of unbelievable events that he claimed had caused his delay. Der. (n.) dubiety, dubiousness; (adv.) dubiously.

duplication - (n.) the action of making copies of an object. e.g. - The teacher realized that the student had copied his homework from his friend since there was some <u>duplication</u> in the mistakes that were made. Der. (v.) duplicate; (adj.) duplicated.

duplicitous - (adj.) relating to living a deceptive or double life. e.g. - The <u>duplicitous</u> man had two wives, neither of whom knew of the other's existence. Der. (adv.) duplicitously.

dwindle - (v.) to decrease in size or amount. e.g. - The size of the class has <u>dwindled</u>. We began with twenty-five students and now have only five. Der. (adj.) dwindling.

dysfunction - (n.) failure to function properly. e.g. - The <u>dysfunction</u> in their relationship caused the couple to file for divorce. Der. (adj.) dysfunctional.

Exercises – D

Instructions: Complete the sentences below, using one of the words beginning with the letter "D" from the previous section. Note that some gaps require a single word, while others may need a phrasal verb or idiomatic expression. You may also need to change the form of the word. The answers are provided at the end of book.

1) A _____ cloud hung overhead, threatening us with rain.

2) The crime of murder is a _____ act.

3) Students must be _____ when filling in the answer sheet to be sure that they put the answers in the correct space.

4) The mechanic _____ the engine of the car in order to repair it.

5) His farm is very _____. He grows crops and also raises various types of animals.

6) Drugs are the _____ of many people, and addiction is a growing problem in our country.

7) There is a high level of _____ in their family. In fact, most of the siblings don't speak to each other.

8) That restaurant was so _____. It appeared that the floor had never been cleaned.

9) I know that you are about to panic, but please don't make a decision in _____.

10) The store was offering a refund to customers because of a _____ in the product they had sold.

Words – E

Instructions: Study the words below, paying attention to their meanings as well as how they are used in the example sentences. Then complete the exercise that follows.

earnest - (adj.) relating to sincerity in character. e.g. - If you are <u>earnest</u> when speaking about your problem, you will certainly receive support and sympathy. (n.) earnestness; (adv.) earnestly.

eerie - (adj.) frightening; scary. e.g. - Why do you watch those <u>eerie</u> films? You know you always feel afraid afterwards. Der. (adv.) eerily.

effigy - (n.) a monument or memorial shaped in the likeness of a particular individual. e.g. - An <u>effigy</u> of a soldier can be found in the centre of many villages.

elaborate - (adj.) developed; containing many details. e.g. - He told such an <u>elaborate</u> story that it was impossible to remember all the details. Der. (n.) elaboration; (v.) elaborate; (adv.) elaborately.

elated - (adj.) very pleased or happy; delighted. e.g. - She was <u>elated</u> when her baby was born. It was the happiest day of her life. Der. (n.) elation; (v.) elate.

elements - (n.) changes in the weather. e.g. - You must dress yourself warmly in the winter to protect yourself against the <u>elements</u>.

elicit - (v.) to bring out; evoke. e.g. - The teacher gave the students many clues in order to <u>elicit</u> the correct answer. Der. (n.) elicitation.

elite - (adj.) relating to a limited group; (syn.) exclusive. e.g. - The Beverly Hills Hotel is used only by an <u>elite</u> group of people, including famous movie stars.

elusive - (adj.) impossible to be accomplished or maintained. e.g. - Her dream of becoming a professional ballet dancer has proved to be <u>elusive</u>. She was rejected at the audition and is now working in a department store. Der. (n.) elusion; (n.) elusiveness; (v.) elude; (adv.) elusively.

ember - (n.) a small glowing fragment which remains when a fire is being extinguished. e.g. - Be careful when removing <u>embers</u> from your fireplace. They may still be burning and should not be thrown on paper garbage.

embezzle - (v.) to use one's own position to steal company money or property for personal use. e.g. - The company's accountant had been <u>embezzling</u> money for years by transferring it from the company's bank to his own personal account. Der. (n.) embezzlement; (adj.) embezzled.

embroil - (v.) to cause to become involved in a conflict. e.g. - She became <u>embroiled</u> in the argument by telling a different version of events.

eminent - (adj.) showing superiority or high achievement in one's profession. e.g. - The professor was <u>eminent</u> in the field of micro-biology and had written several well-known books on the subject.

emission - (n.) to give off or send out light, sound, or smell. e.g. The emission of poisonous gases into the atmosphere is illegal. Der. (v.) emit.

emulate - (v.) to imitate or equal in quality. e.g. - Your brother is a perfect child. You should try to emulate him. Der. (n.) emulation; (adj.) emulate.

encompass - (v.) to involve or include. (syn.) encompass e.g. - Business Studies encompass the subjects of marketing and economics.

encounter - (v.) to meet or come across. e.g. - I encountered Jane in the shopping mall, although we hadn't arranged to meet. Der. (n.) encounter.

endeavour - (v.) to attempt with difficulty. e.g. - The doctor will endeavour to see you this afternoon, although his schedule is quite full. Der. (n.) endeavour.

endorse - (v.) to openly express approval or support; (syn.) back. e.g. - The budget reductions that the manager proposed were not endorsed by the company. Der. (n.) endorsement; (adj.) endorsed.

endowment - (n.) grant or contribution of money for support of an activity. e.g. - The millionaire contributed a substantial endowment towards the building of the new hospital. Der. (v.) endow; (adj.) endowed.

enervating - (adj.) exhausting. e.g. - Running a marathon is an enervating experience and requires several days of rest afterwards. Der. (n.) enervate.

engulf - (v.) to be consumed totally by fire. e.g. - The fire department could not save the building since it was already engulfed in flames when they arrived.

enhance - (v.) to make something greater or more beautiful. e.g. - Some people have plastic surgery in order to enhance their appearance. Der. (n.) enhancement; (adj.) enhanced.

enmity - (n.) hatred; (syn.) contempt. e.g. - They hardly parted as friends. In fact, I'd say she feels enmity towards him.

ensign - (n.) a flag which indicates nationality; (syn.) banner. e.g. - The ensign of Great Britain is red, white, and blue.

entail - (v.) to involve or include. e.g. - Sarah's new job as manager entails many responsibilities.

enterprise - (n.) a business organization established for a particular purpose or activity. e.g. - Banks and insurance companies are business enterprises. Der. (adj.) enterprising.

enthral - (v.) to totally attract the attention of someone; to charm. e.g. - She was totally enthralled with the charm of the Canary Islands and would like to go there again next summer. Der. (adj.) enthralling; (n.) enthrallment.

entice - (v.) to attract by persuasion or influence. e.g. - The advertisement in the store window enticed him to go inside. Der. (n.) enticement; (adj.) enticing.

entity - (n.) a business or enterprise. e.g. - A partnership is one type of business <u>entity</u>.

entreat - (v.) to beg; (syn.) beseech; implore. e.g. - The organization <u>entreated</u> the public to give donations to charity. Der. (n.) entreaty.

equivocation - (n.) the action of speaking in a way that is likely to cause confusion or misunderstanding. e.g. - The lawyer spoke with <u>equivocation</u>, saying that the product was not dangerous, nor was it safe. Der. (v.) equivocate; (adj.) equivocal; (adv.) equivocally; (ant.) unequivocal.

era - (n.) a period in history. e.g. - The Middle Ages were a particular <u>era</u> in history.

erratic - (adj.) unpredictable; inconsistent. e.g. - Her moods are so <u>erratic</u>. You never know if she'll be happy or upset. Der. (adv.) erratically.

escort - (v.) to go along with; (syn.) accompany. e.g. - Rachel's father <u>escorted</u> her on her first date. She was so embarrassed to be seen with him. Der. (n.) escort.

esteem - (n.) value or appreciation. e.g. - You are totally lacking in self-<u>esteem</u>. You should really think more highly of yourself. Der. (v.) esteem.

estuary - (n.) the mouth of a river or other waterway. e.g. - The River Thames flows to its <u>estuary</u> in Essex.

eternal - (adj.) lasting forever. e.g. - Guess what? My boyfriend declared his <u>eternal</u> love for me last night. He said he'd love me forever. Der. (n.) eternity; (adv.) eternally.

exacerbate - (v.) to make worse or more severe. e.g. - He <u>exacerbated</u> the fire by throwing petrol on it. Der. (n.) exacerbation.

exaggerate - (v.) to overstate in size or amount. e.g. - The fisherman <u>exaggerated</u> by saying that he had caught a twelve pound fish when, in fact, it weighed only six pounds. Der. (n.) exaggeration; (adj.) exaggerated; (adv.) exaggeratedly.

exalt - (v.) to give praise and glory. e.g. - The soldier was <u>exalted</u> for the bravery he displayed in battle.

exasperation - (n.) a state of extreme irritation or annoyance. e.g. - He felt <u>exasperation</u> when the building collapsed while he was just finishing the repairs. Der. (v.) exasperate; (adj.) exasperated, exasperating; (adv.) exasperatingly.

exclusive - (adj.) capable of use or possession only by a limited group. e.g. - The <u>exclusive</u> news report was broadcast only by one channel. Der. (n.) exclusivity; (v.) exclude; (adv.) exclusively.

exertion - (n.) excessive physical activity. e.g. - Much <u>exertion</u> was required to climb the mountain. Afterwards, the climbers were exhausted. Der. (v.) exert; (adj.) exerting.

exhale - (v.) to expel air out by breathing. e.g. - He <u>exhaled</u> the cigarette smoke by breathing it out of his nose and mouth. Der. (n.) exhalation.

exhaust - (n.) the expenditure of gas from a machine. e.g. - The <u>exhaust</u> from automobiles has caused environmental problems in all major European cities.

exile - (v.) to expel or force to leave, esp. one's country of origin. e.g. - She was <u>exiled</u> from government office due to her political viewpoints. Der. (n.) exile.

exonerate - (v.) to clear from accusation or responsibility. e.g. - A finding of "not guilty" <u>exonerates</u> a suspect from all responsibility for a crime. Der. (n.) exoneration.

exorbitant - (adj.) excessive in quantity or price; (syn.) extortionate. e.g. - You paid $5 for a candy bar. What an <u>exorbitant</u> price. Der. (n.) exorbitance; (adv.) exorbitantly.

expel - (v.) to force to leave school, usually for misbehaviour. e.g. - He was <u>expelled</u> from high school for starting a fire in the classroom. Der. (n.) expulsion; (adj.) expelled.

exploit - (v.) to use or manipulate another person for one's own purposes. e.g. - Don't let him <u>exploit</u> you. He's only using you for money and a place to stay. Der. (n.) exploitation.

extenuating - (adj.) relating to lessening the seriousness of a charge; mitigating. e.g. - The use of self-defence is an <u>extenuating</u> circumstance against the charge of murder. Der. (v.) extenuate.

extermination - (n.) the action of killing insects or rodents. e.g. - After discovering several mice in our kitchen, it was necessary to call a company into our home for <u>extermination</u>. Der. (v.) exterminate.

extortionate - (adj.) excessively expensive; (syn.) exorbitant. e.g. - He paid the <u>extortionate</u> price of £5000 for a pair of tennis shoes. Der. (adv.) extortionately.

extract - (v.) to remove. e.g. - The information you need can be <u>extracted</u> from this book. Der. (n.) extract, extraction; (adj.) extracted.

extravagant - (adj.) unnecessarily high in price or expense. e.g. - Giving your girlfriend a new car for her birthday was too <u>extravagant</u>. You should have given her a much cheaper present. Der. (n.) extravagance.

Exercises – E

Instructions: Complete the sentences below, using one of the words beginning with the letter "E" from the previous section. Note that some gaps require a single word, while others may need a phrasal verb or idiomatic expression. You may also need to change the form of the word. The answers are provided at the end of book.

1) Success proved to be _____ to him, and he couldn't realize his dream of becoming a professional football player.

2) The last few weeks of the semester are _____. I get very little sleep because I am preparing so many assignments and essays.

3) The business _____ had corporate offices in the same building.

4) I know she is angry at you, but don't _____ the situation by telling her that she is foolish.

5) You can get an excused absence from class if there are _____ circumstances.

6) Preparing for a party _____ many small details.

7) An _____ of the man who founded the town can be found in the park.

8) That street has an _____ atmosphere after dark, and many people avoid it because they are afraid.

9) The manager was fired for _____ from the company bank account.

10) I will _____ to get into an advanced English class, although I may not succeed.

Words – F

Instructions: Study the words below, paying attention to their meanings as well as how they are used in the example sentences. Then complete the exercise that follows.

fable - (n.) a story based on magical happenings. e.g. - That story is a <u>fable</u> because it's not possible for a frog to turn into a handsome prince.

fabricate - (v.) manufacture; (syn.) assemble. e.g. - Alfonso <u>fabricated</u> a huge story which was made of lies. Der. (n.) fabrication; (adj.) fabricated.

face the music - (id.) to accept reality. e.g. - <u>Face the music</u>! Your girlfriend isn't coming back to you!

facetious - (adj.) relating to inappropriate humour or jokes. e.g. - When I said that Tom Cruise was my cousin, I was only being <u>facetious</u>. I never thought that you would take me seriously. Der. (adv.) facetiously.

fad - (n.) an attraction or fashion existing for a short period of time with overwhelming interest. e.g. - Bell-bottomed jeans were a <u>fad</u> in the 1960's.

fade - (v.) to gradually lose colour. e.g. - Blue jeans <u>fade</u> after repeated washing and become lighter in colour. Der. (adj.) faded.

fair-weather friend - (id.) loyal only during times of good fortune. e.g. - Don't trust him. He's a <u>fair-weather</u> friend.

fallacious - (adj.) incorrect as a result of being based on false theories or beliefs. e.g. - The theory that the earth is flat is totally <u>fallacious</u>. Der. (n.) fallacy; (adv.) fallaciously.

fatality - (n.) a death caused by an accident or natural disaster. e.g. - Three <u>fatalities</u> resulted from the road accident. A man, woman, and child were reported dead. Der. (adj.) fatal; (adv.) fatally.

fathom - (v.) to understand or comprehend, esp. with difficulty. e.g. - I can't <u>fathom</u> this chemistry homework. Can you explain it to me? Der. (adj.) fathomable; (ant.) unfathomable.

feat - (n.) accomplishment. e.g. - Receiving a university degree by the age of thirteen is quite an amazing <u>feat</u>.

feeble - (adj.) lacking in strength, esp. as a result of old age. e.g. - Anne's grandmother is quite <u>feeble</u> and cannot lift heavy objects. Der. (adv.) feebly.

feel together - (id.) to feel organised and well. e.g. - I wouldn't approach your boss for a raise today. She can't be <u>feeling together</u> after the way she drank at the party last night.

fellowship - (adj.) relating to the gathering of individual members in a group or society. e.g. - The <u>fellowship</u> of Veterans of Former Wars gathers once a month for a meeting in the town hall.

fertilizer - (n.) chemicals applied to planted fields to enhance growth and increase production. e.g. - Health conscious people prefer naturally-grown organic vegetables as they believe that the <u>fertilizers</u> placed on other vegetables are harmful to the health. Der. (v.) fertilize; (adj.) fertile; (adj.) fertilized.

fervid - (adj.) showing extreme enthusiasm or passion. e.g. - He is a <u>fervid</u> fan of the local football team. He never misses a game.

fetter - (v.)(met.) to restrict; to prevent the progress of. e.g. - Being the mother of four young children, she is <u>fettered</u> with responsibility. Der. (n.) fetter.

fib - (v.) to lie. e.g. - He <u>fibbed</u> about being related to the President. Der. (n.) fib.

fickle - (adj.) changeable or inconstant; capricious. e.g. - She is a very <u>fickle</u> girl and constantly changes her mind.

fidget - (v.) to sit restlessly. e.g. - Young children often <u>fidget</u> if they have been sitting in one place for too long. Der. (adj.) fidgeting.

figure - (v.)(met.) to think or believe; reckon. e.g. - I <u>figure</u> that he's lying because his story doesn't make sense.

figure – (1)(n.) the shape of a person's body; (2)(n.) amount; number. e.g. - (1) Your <u>figure</u> would be better if you went on a diet. (2) The latest <u>figures</u> indicate that the population of our city is now 10,000. Der. (v.) figure.

figure out - (ph. v.) to attempt to understand. e.g. - I can't <u>figure out</u> my math homework.

fizzle out - (id.) to reduce gradually in amount or quality. e.g. - Interest in our exercise class has <u>fizzled out</u>. There are only two students left.

flank - (v.) to be located on both sides of someone or something. e.g. - Our house is <u>flanked</u> by a grocery store on the east and a parking lot on the west.

flap - (n.) a piece of paper or cardboard which is placed over an adjoining piece. e.g. - You must moisten the <u>flap</u> in order to seal the back of the envelope.

flaunt - (v.) to show or display something obviously or pretentiously. e.g. - She <u>flaunted</u> her new diamond ring by waving her hand in front of my face. Der. (adj.) flaunted.

flaw - (n.) an imperfection in appearance or function. e.g. - The jacket had a serious <u>flaw</u> since one sleeve was longer than the other. Der. (adj.) flawed.

flicker - (n.) a small flame. e.g. - The <u>flicker</u> from the candle provided enough light to see in the dark room. Der. (v.) flicker.

flinch - (v.) to experience involuntary spasms as a result of pain. e.g. - The man's legs <u>flinched</u> and jerked when they were crushed in the accident. Der. (n.) flinch.

flirt with disaster - (id.) to become involved in a dangerous or risky situation. e.g. - Every time you drive over the speed limit, you are just <u>flirting with disaster</u>.

flock - (n.) a group of animals, such as sheep or birds. e.g. - The <u>flock</u> of sheep was gathered at the north end of the field. Der. (v.) flock.

flog a dead horse - (id.) to waste effort talking about a situation that cannot be changed. e.g. - My classmate is always talking about failing her exams. She is <u>flogging a dead horse</u>.

flop - (n.)(met.) a complete and total lack of success. e.g. - His business was a <u>flop</u> because he didn't know how to manage his money.

flounder - (v.) to work without obtaining results; to struggle. e.g. - Chris really <u>floundered</u> during his first few weeks on the job since his boss did not provide any instructions or assistance. Der. (adj.) floundering.

flourish - (v.) to reach the highest state of activity or development. e.g. - Flowers <u>flourish</u> if they are grown in the warmth of a greenhouse.

fluctuate - (v.) to change back and forth. e.g. - The weather often <u>fluctuates</u> from hot to cold at this time of year. Der. (n.) fluctuation.

fodder - (n.) animal food. e.g. - The horse was in the stable, eating his <u>fodder</u>.

foil - (v.) to thwart or prevent the progress of. e.g. - The bank robber's plan was <u>foiled</u> when the security alarm went off. Der. (adj.) foiled.

folklore - (n.) traditional stories. e.g.- Some books are based on fact. Others are based on <u>folklore</u>.

for all intents and purposes - (id.) for all practical purposes; in effect. e.g. - My computer is useless <u>for all intents and purposes</u> since I cannot use new software on it.

for keeps - (id.) to take possession or ownership of sthg forever. e.g. - He gave me a diamond ring <u>for keeps</u>.

forage - (v.) to search for something, esp. in the countryside. e.g. - She was <u>foraging</u> in her disorganized closet, looking for her favourite pair of shoes.

forecast - (v.) to predict; to estimate. e.g. - The meteorologist <u>forecasts</u> snow for tomorrow. Der. (n.) forecast.

foremost - (adj.) the most important or noteworthy. e.g. - First and <u>foremost</u>, you must always be honest.

forerunner - (n.) current authority or leader. e.g. - Coca-Cola is a <u>forerunner</u> in the soft drink industry.

forlorn - (adj.) loneliness and despair; (syn.) desolate. e.g. - He felt <u>forlorn</u> after his wife filed for divorce. Der. (n.) forlornness; (adv.) forlornly.

fortitude - (n.) strength; courage. e.g. - He showed great <u>fortitude</u> in saving the drowning man from the raging river. Der. (v.) fortify; (adj.) fortified.

fortuitous - (adj.) happening by chance or accident; unplanned. e.g. - I had a <u>fortuitous</u> meeting with an old friend today. By coincidence, we both happened to be in the doctor's office at the same time. Der. (adv.) fortuitously.

foster - (v.) to adopt or encourage; nurture. e.g. - You'd feel more optimistic if you <u>fostered</u> a positive attitude.

fraction - (n.) a part or percentage of the whole. e.g. - He ate only a <u>fraction</u> of the pie. Three-quarters of it is left. Der. (v.) fractionalize; (adj.) fractional; (adv.) fractionally.

fracture - (n.) a broken bone. e.g. - Tom had many <u>fractures</u> as a result of the car accident. Der. (v.) fracture; (adj.) fractured.

frail - (adj.) being easily broken; weak. e.g. - Elderly people suffer from <u>frail</u> bones that can break easily. Der. (n.) frailty; (adv.) frailly.

fraudulent - (adj.) based on trickery or dishonesty. e.g. - His offer to make you president of his company is entirely <u>fraudulent</u> since no such company exists. Der. (n.) fraud; (adv.) fraudulently.

fraught - (adj.) to be full of something. e.g. - He is <u>fraught</u> with nervousness these days about his upcoming wedding.

fresh out of sthg - (id.) to have exhausted the supply of something. e.g. - We are <u>fresh out of</u> grapefruit today ma'am. You'll need to come back again tomorrow.

fret - (v.) to be anxious with worry. e.g. - Joanne has been <u>fretting</u> about her exam results. She is worried that she might have failed. Der. (n.) fret.

frigid - (adj.) extremely cold; freezing. e.g. - The <u>frigid</u> weather caused the plants to freeze. Der. (n.) frigidity; (adv.) frigidly.

frivolous - (adj.) without seriousness or importance. e.g. - Don't you think it was <u>frivolous</u> of her to complain about losing such a small amount of money?

frolic - (v.) to run and play freely. e.g. - The children were <u>frolicking</u> in the playground. Der. (n.) frolic; (adj.) frolicsome.

frontier - (n.) an unclaimed or unsettled area or territory. e.g. - Outer space is an unexplored <u>frontier</u>

frugal - (adj.) to be very restrictive with money or in spending. e.g. - Isabel is very <u>frugal</u> as she is living on a pension.

fruitful - (adj.) relating to something which is very productive. e.g. - I had a <u>fruitful</u> afternoon at the office. I finished all of my work. Der. (adv.) fruitfully.

fugitive - (n.) an individual who has escaped or is running from the law. e.g. - Charles escaped from prison five years ago and now lives his life hiding as a <u>fugitive</u>.

fulsome - (adj.) abundant or excessive. e.g. - He received <u>fulsome</u> praise for returning the lost ten dollars. Der. (n.) fulsomeness; (adv.) fulsomely.

fumbling - (adj.) failing to obtain the desired result; (syn.) floundering. e.g. - He made many <u>fumbling</u> attempts, but was never successful. Der. (v.) fumble.

fume - (1)(n.) vapour; (syn.) exhaust; (2)(met.)(v.) to be very angry. e.g. (1) - The odour from this paint is so strong that I am getting a headache from the <u>fumes</u>. (2) He was <u>fuming</u> after I insulted him.

fundamental - (adj.) basic; (syn.) rudimentary. e.g. - The law of gravity is one of the <u>fundamental</u> rules of physics. Der. (adv.) fundamentally.

Exercises – F

Instructions: Complete the sentences below, using one of the words beginning with the letter "F" from the previous section. Note that some gaps require a single word, while others may need a phrasal verb or idiomatic expression. You may also need to change the form of the word. The answers are provided at the end of book.

1) She was being _____. She didn't mean what she said.

2) The soldier was _____ by a comrade on his right and another on his left.

3) I had a _____ encounter with my cousin at the mall today. It was such a coincidence. I didn't even know she was going shopping.

4) It is _____ to complain about such a small, insignificant problem.

5) The _____ principles of geometry state that a right angle will always have ninety degrees.

6) The orchestra paid _____ tribute to the composer by playing all of his concertos.

7) Children _____ if given love, care, discipline, and support.

8) Our plans for vacation were _____ when a hurricane hit the resort area.

9) The horses were _____ in the field, running around playfully with one another.

10) Attendance at yoga will _____ if the instructor fails to make the class interesting or useful.

Words – G to H

Instructions: Study the words below, paying attention to their meanings as well as how they are used in the example sentences. Then complete the exercise that follows.

gait - (n.) an individual's style of running, walking, or stepping. e.g. - He finished the race first because he ran with the fastest gait.

garbled - (adj.) confused or unclear in meaning. e.g. - He left a garbled message that no one could understand. Der. (v.) garble.

garish - (adj.) the quality of being displayed excessively or tastelessly. e.g. - The interior decorations of their house were garish: red carpeting, orange curtains, and a purple sofa. Der. (adv.) garishly.

garnish - (n.) fruit or vegetable pieces added to food or drinks to enhance their appearance. e.g. - Slices of lemon or orange are used as garnishes for dishes served in restaurants. Der. (v.) garnish.

garrulous - (adj.) talkative; outgoing; (syn.) gregarious, ebullient. e.g. - He is so garrulous that sometimes it's difficult to make him stop talking. Der. (adv.) garrulously.

gash - (n.) a long, deep cut. e.g. - He got a gash on his finger when the knife he was using to cut the cheese slipped from his hand. Der. (v.) gash.

gauge - (n.) a small machine which is used for measuring. e.g. - The gauge on this machine will measure the air pressure inside the tires. Der. (v.) gauge.

gear (towards) - (v.) to make to satisfy a certain condition. e.g. - The style of clothes in that store is geared towards teenagers. You won't be able to find a gift for your mother there. Der. (n.) gear.

genial - (adj.) polite, well-mannered. e.g. - He is very genial. Not once have I heard him speak in a rude or impolite way. Der. (adv.) genially.

get on like cats and dogs - (id.) to be entirely incompatible. e.g. - I can't live with my mother. We get on like cats and dogs.

get in touch - (id.) to get in contact with someone. e.g. - Get in touch with me next week. You can telephone me at home.

get on sbdy's good side - (id.) to win someone's favor. e.g. - He tried to get on the teacher's good side by bringing her gifts.

get the lowdown on something - (id.) to obtain secret or inside information about something. e.g. - Did you get the lowdown? I heard a rumour that the factory is going to close.

gimmick - (n.) a trick or feature used to attract to attention. e.g. - Free gifts or samples are often included with new products as a gimmick to entice the customer to buy them.

give sbdy a lift - (id.) to give someone a ride in your car. e.g. - Can you <u>give me a lift</u> into town?

give sbdy the creeps - (id.) to frighten someone. e.g. - Horror movies <u>give me the creeps</u>.

give sbdy a break - (id.) to stop giving harsh treatment to an individual. e.g. - What do you mean? You won't help me! <u>Give me a break</u>!

glum - (adj.) without hope; depressed. e.g. - Bruce is really <u>glum</u> these days. He is unhappy about failing his exams again. Der. (adv.) glumly.

gnaw - (v.) to chew on, esp. continuously. e.g. - The rats were <u>gnawing</u> on the wood with their teeth.

go-ahead - (n.) a gesture of authority or approval. e.g. - After weeks of refusing, the manager finally gave the <u>go-ahead</u> for the project.

gobble - (v.) to eat quickly or greedily. e.g. - He <u>gobbled</u> the food like a pig and got a stomach ache from eating so quickly.

go-between - (n.) an individual who makes arrangements or mediates. e.g. - He acted as a <u>go-between</u> in arranging the blind date for his two friends. Der. (ph. v.) go between.

gorgeous - (adj.) very beautiful; stunning. e.g. - The winner of the beauty contest was a very <u>gorgeous</u> woman.

grab a bite - (id.) to go for a meal, esp. quickly. e.g. - Let's <u>grab a bite</u> for lunch.

grain - (n.) seeds of cereal plants, such as corn or wheat. e.g. - Food products such as rice and corn are <u>grains</u>.

grasp - (1)(v.) to hold or embrace with the hands or arms; (syn.) clasp, clutch; (2)(met.) to understand. e.g. - (1) Mary stood at the bus stop, <u>grasping</u> her bags in her hands. (2) I can't <u>grasp</u> what you are saying. Can you please explain it to me again? Der. (n.) grasp.

grasping at straws - (id.) to try many alternative solutions in desperation. e.g. - You don't know the answer to the homework so now you're <u>grasping at straws</u>.

graze - (v.) to feed on grass. e.g. - The sheep were <u>grazing</u> in the meadow, eating grass.

green - (id.) inexperienced; without knowledge. e.g. – The new employee is <u>green</u> since today is his first day on the job, and he has no previous experience.

grimy - (adj.) dirty; filthy. e.g. - They live like pigs. Their house is so <u>grimy</u>. Der. (n.) grime.

grove - (n.) a small group of trees, which often bear fruit or nuts. e.g. - We have a small <u>grove</u> of pine trees in our front yard.

grow on - (id.) to get used to. e.g. - I didn't like my new school too much at first, but it has started to <u>grow on</u> me.

grumble - (v.) to complain; (syn.) whine. e.g. - There is no reason to <u>grumble</u> about your job. If you don't like it, find a new one. Der. (n.) grumble.

haggle (with) - (v.) to engage in discussions with buyers or sellers in order to agree upon a price; negotiate. e.g. - He <u>haggled</u> with the car salesman in order to negotiate a good price.

hamlet - (n.) a small town or village. e.g. - Two-hundred years ago, Newcastle was a small <u>hamlet</u>, but now it's a huge city.

handle sthg - (id.) to endure or tolerate something. e.g. - I just can't <u>handle</u> waking up so early in the morning.

handy - (adj.) near at hand; easy to use; convenient. e.g. - The neighbourhood convenience store is <u>handy</u> because it's very close to our house.

harvest - (v.) to gather produce from a field. e.g. - The farmer <u>harvested</u> the apples in the fall by picking them from the trees. Der. (n.) harvest.

haughty - (adj.) overly proud. e.g. - She was <u>haughty</u> about winning first prize in the contest. Der. (adv.) haughtily.

haunted - (adj.) relating to places that are believed to be occupied by ghosts or spirits of the dead. e.g. - Many people believe that spirits of the dead <u>haunt</u> graveyards. Der. (v.) haunt.

have a one-track mind - (id.) to only have one thing on your mind. e.g. - She <u>has a one-track mind</u>. All she ever thinks about is money.

have pull - (id.) to be influential. e.g. - I think he can get us tickets for the match on Sunday. He <u>has pull</u> with the team.

He made his bed, and now he can lie in it. - (id.) a person must face the consequences of his or her actions. e.g. - It was his own decision to cheat on the exam. Now that he got caught, I can only say that <u>he made his bed, and now he can lie in it</u>.

heard it through the grapevine - (id.) to hear some people talking or gossiping about a subject. e.g. - I wasn't told the news about the situation directly. I <u>heard it through the grapevine</u>.

hearth - (n.) the floor of a fireplace. e.g. - The fire was burning in the <u>hearth</u>.

hearty - (adj.) relating to physical strength and good health; (syn.) strapping. e.g. - Regular exercise and healthy food will make you <u>hearty</u>. Der. (n.) heartiness; (adv.) heartily.

hectic - (adj.) exceptionally active or busy. e.g. - What a <u>hectic</u> day. I haven't had a moment to rest. Der. (adv.) hectically.

heinous - (adj.) exceptionally shocking or horrible. e.g. - The murder of the young children was a <u>heinous</u> crime and should be punished severely.

hilarious - (adj.) very funny or humorous. e.g. - She told a <u>hilarious</u> story, which caused everyone to break out into fits of laughter. Der. (n.) hilarity; (adv.) hilariously.

hindrance - (n.) the action of holding back, delaying, or preventing the progress of something; (syn.) obstacle; stumbling block. e.g. - His constant interruptions were a <u>hindrance</u> to the completion of the job. Der. (v.) hinder.

hindsight - (n.) the understanding of the consequences of an event after it has occurred. e.g. - With <u>hindsight</u>, he realizes the mistakes he has made in his past.

hit the nail on the head - (id.) to make an appropriate remark or statement. e.g. - The politician <u>hit the nail on the head</u> when he said that more financial aid should be offered to students.

Hit the road! - (id.) Go away. Leave me alone. (syn.) Take a hike! e.g. - A strange man was bothering me in the mall so I told him to <u>hit the road</u>.

hit the spot - (id.) That was just what I was craving. e.g. - Lemonade really <u>hits the spot</u> on a hot summer day.

hoarse - (adj.) unpleasant or rough in sound. e.g. – My brother is <u>hoarse</u> from shouting too much at the football game last night. Der. (adv.) hoarsely.

hoax - (n.) a fictitious report of a sighting or event. e.g. - His report of viewing an aircraft from outer-space was a total <u>hoax</u>.

hold a grudge - (id.) to bear resentment towards another person. e.g. - Julia is still <u>holding a grudge</u> because I criticized her work.

hold your tongue - (id.) to keep one's opinions to oneself. e.g. - I wanted to tell her off, but I <u>held my tongue</u>.

hollow - (adj.) relating to objects that are not solid in content. e.g. - The children were disappointed that the candy was <u>hollow</u> and did not have a filling in the center. Der. (n.) hollow, hollowness; (v.) hollow; (adv.) hollowly.

hop in - (id.) get inside my car. e.g. - I'll take you to the store. <u>Hop in</u>.

How come? - (id.) Why? e.g. - She's not going out tonight. <u>How come</u>?

hunch - (n.) an instinctive feeling or idea. e.g. - I didn't have any proof that he was lying. It was only a <u>hunch</u>.

hurl - (v.) to throw with great force or strength. e.g. - The rugby player <u>hurled</u> the ball to his teammate, who caught it.

hushed - (adj.) quiet; subdued. e.g. - The examination hall was <u>hushed</u> as the students were writing. It was so quiet that you could hear a pin drop. Der. (v.) hush. Der. (n.) hush.

Exercises – G to H

Instructions: Complete the sentences below, using one of the words beginning with the letters "G" or "H" from the previous section. Note that some gaps require a single word, while others may need a phrasal verb or idiomatic expression. You may also need to change the form of the word. The answers are provided at the end of book.

1) If you should have any questions or complaints, please _____ with the manager of the company.

2) Parsley or mint are often used as _____ for meat dishes.

3) The nursery school is _____ because it's less than a mile from my home.

4) She _____ constantly about her boyfriend. If she is so unhappy, she should leave him.

5) You don't know how to respond to the accusation, so now you are _____.

6) If you shout too much you will become _____.

7) That meal really _____. I was craving a pizza.

8) The police officer didn't have any evidence to charge the suspect with the crime. He only had a _____.

9) The instructions were _____ , so we couldn't understand what we needed to do.

10) The auditorium was _____ as the Vice Chancellor was about to begin her speech.

Words – I

Instructions: Study the words below, paying attention to their meanings as well as how they are used in the example sentences. Then complete the exercise that follows.

idle - (adj.) inactive or non-functioning. e.g. - The plant is closed because it is <u>idle</u> this month.

ignite - (v.) to start a fire. e.g. - The police investigation determined that the fire had been <u>ignited</u> with gasoline. Der. (n.) ignition.

illicit - (adj.) illegal. e.g. - <u>Illicit</u> drugs, such as heroin and cocaine, have become a serious problem of modern society. Der. (adv.) illicitly.

immaculate - (adj.) exceptionally clean or tidy. e.g. - Her house was so <u>immaculate</u> that no dust or dirt could be seen. Der. (adv.) immaculately.

immature - (adj.) childish. e.g. - Although my brother is 50 years old, he is <u>immature</u> and behaves like a child. Der. (n.) immaturity; (ant.) mature.

immense - (adj.) huge or extensive. e.g. - You wrote a 2,000 page book. That must have required an <u>immense</u> amount of work. Der. (adv.) immensely.

impact - (n.) effect; consequence. e.g. - Your failure to work hard now will have a negative <u>impact</u> on your future. Der. (v.) impact.

impartial - (adj.) relating to treatment with fairness and equality; unbiased. e.g. - An <u>impartial</u> teacher does not have favourite students, but treats all students equally. Der. (n.) impartiality; (adv.) impartially.

impeccable - (adj.) without fault or blame; perfect. e.g. - I don't believe his behaviour is as <u>impeccable</u> as you say. Nobody's perfect, you know. Der. (adv.) impeccably.

imperative - (adj.) essential; exceptionally urgent or important. e.g. - It is <u>imperative</u> that this medicine be taken exactly every eight hours. Failure to do so can result in death.

implement - (n.) a tool or piece of equipment used for a specific purpose. e.g. - Several <u>implements</u>, such as ploughs, are needed to harvest crops from the fields in the fall. Der. (n.) implementation; (v.) implement.

implicate - (v.) to show proof of the commission of or involvement in a crime; (syn.) incriminate. e.g. - His possession of the gun used in the murder <u>implicated</u> him in the crime. Der. (n.) implication.

implore - (v.) to beg; (syn.) entreat, beseech. e.g. - The Prime Minister <u>implored</u> the nation for its support during the country's economic crisis. Der. (adj.) imploring; (adv.) imploringly.

imposing - (adj.) overwhelming in size or amount. e.g. – A flat in Belgravia can cost well over £1,000,000, which is far too <u>imposing</u> for most people. Der. (v.) impose.

impregnable - (adj.) incapable of being entered or penetrated. e.g. - The castle was impregnable and could not be invaded by the enemy. Der. (n.) impregnability; (adv.) impregnably.

impropriety - (n.) improper behaviour. e.g. - I can't believe you had the impropriety to flirt with your boss's wife. Der. (ant.) propriety.

in the red - (id.) to have a negative numerical balance. e.g. - The company had to close down after operating in the red for months.

incidental - (adj.) not relating to the main part; minor. e.g. - Your comments are only incidental and will not have an effect on our final decision. Der. (adv.) incidentally.

incongruity - (n.) incompatibility or disagreement between or among things. e.g. - There is total incongruity between the lies he told and reality. Der. (adj.) incongruous; (ant.) congruity.

incriminate - (v.) to show proof concerning the commission of or involvement in a crime; (syn.) implicate. e.g. - The presence of the attacker's blood type at the murder scene incriminated him in the crime. Der. (n.) incrimination; (adj.) incriminating.

indefatigable - (adj.) incapable of experiencing fatigue or exhaustion. e.g. - My boss is indefatigable. He never gets tired and is always energetic. Der. (adv.) indefatigably.

indigent - (adj.) living in conditions of poverty. e.g. - Without a home or a job, she is indigent and is living on the streets. Der. (n.) indigence.

indignant - (adj.) feeling anger as a result of being unfairly accused of a wrongdoing. e.g. - He became indignant when his wife wrongly accused him of cheating on her. Der. (n.) indignity; (adv.) indignantly.

indispensable - (adj.) essential; necessary. e.g. - Fresh food and water are indispensable for human survival. Der. (n.) indispensability; (adv.) indispensably.

indulge - (v.) to enjoy sthg without discipline, control, or restraint. e.g. - If you indulge in too much food, you will become fat. Der. (n.) indulgence; (adj.) indulgent; (adv.) indulgently.

industrious - (adj.) relating to very hard-working individuals. e.g. – The manager received a promotion because he was so industrious.

infirmity - (n.) the condition of being weak as a result of illness, injury, or disease. e.g. - His broken leg has never healed properly. This infirmity causes him great pain, especially when walking. Der. (adj.) infirm.

infringement - (n.)(syn.) violation. e.g. - Cheating on examinations is an infringement of the academic integrity policy of the university. Der. (v.) infringe.

infuriate - (v.) to cause to become extremely angry. e.g. - Your comment that I am stupid really infuriates me! Der. (n.) fury; (adj.) furious.

ingenious - (adj.) exceptionally intelligent, intellectual, or inventive. e.g. - Men such as Einstein and Edison were highly <u>ingenious</u>.

inhabitant - (n.) resident. e.g. - He has been an <u>inhabitant</u> of Boston for the past fifteen years. Der. (v.) inhabit.

inhale - (v.) to draw air in by breathing. e.g. - He <u>inhaled</u> the cigarette smoke deep into his lungs. Der. (n.) inhalation.

inheritance - (n.) the action of receiving money or specific property upon another person's death. e.g. - James received a substantial <u>inheritance</u> when his parents died, and he is now quite rich. Der. (v.) inherit.

inimical - (adj.) harmful or adverse; hostile. e.g. - The United Nations attempts to improve <u>inimical</u> relationships among various countries through goodwill and diplomacy. Der. (adv.) inimically.

innate - (adj.) inborn; inherent. e.g. - She has <u>innate</u> musical talent and learned how to play the piano in only two days. Der. (adv.) innately.

innocuous - (adj.) not causing harm or injury. e.g. - That snake is not poisonous. In fact, it is totally <u>innocuous</u>.

innovative - (adj.) new; novel. e.g. - This <u>innovative</u> machine is bound to replace every similar older machine currently on the market. Der. (n.) innovation; (v.) innovate.

inquisition - (n.) the process of subjecting to questioning, esp. extensively; (syn.) interrogation. e.g. - Your mother subjected me to an <u>inquisition</u>. I have never been asked so many questions in my life. Der. (adj.) inquisitive; (adv.) inquisitively.

insinuation - (n.) sthg that is implied, inferred, or expressed indirectly. e.g. - His <u>insinuation</u> in saying that I never attended college was that I was stupid. Der. (v.) insinuate.

insolent - (adj.) exhibiting a lack of respect; impudent. e.g. - The <u>insolent</u> student told the teacher that he was stupid. Der. (n.) insolence.

inspiration - (n.) the action of receiving a profound influence, esp. of a spiritual or creative nature. e.g. - The love and support of her husband were an <u>inspiration</u> to her and helped her to write several romance novels. Der. (v.) inspire; (adj.) inspired, inspiring.

installation - (n.) the action of preparing something for use by setting it up in the designated place. e.g. - The <u>installation</u> of your dishwasher is best handled by a plumber. Der. (v.) install.

instigate - (v.) to cause or incite improper or destructive behaviour. e.g. - The leader of the gang <u>instigated</u> his followers into starting the riot. Der. (n.) instigation.

insulation - (1)(n.) the action of preventing the discharge of electricity or loss of heat; (2)(n.)(met.) - the action of offering an individual protection from the consequences of their actions. e.g. - (1) <u>Insulation</u> was placed in the walls of the building in order to ensure warmth in the winter. (2) The criminal received <u>insulation</u> from liability after offering a bribe to the judge. Der. (v.) insulate; (adj.) insulated.

insuperable - (adj.) incapable of being surpassed or overcome; (syn.) insurmountable. e.g. - The problem with this computer system is <u>insuperable</u>. We have no choice but to abandon it and start over from the beginning. Der. (adv.) insuperably.

insurmountable - (adj.) incapable of being passed or overcome; (syn.) insuperable. e.g. - His problems seemed <u>insurmountable</u> and in desperation, he felt that he could not go on. Der. (adv.) insurmountably.

interrogation - (n.) questioning; (syn.) inquisition. e.g. - A full <u>interrogation</u> was conducted to determine the whereabouts of the stolen diamond. Der. (v.) interrogate.

intertwine (with) - (v.)(met.) to become mutually involved in. e.g. - He became <u>intertwined</u> with crime when he agreed to participate in the robbery.

intrepid - (adj.) brave; courageous; unafraid. e.g. - The <u>intrepid</u> explorers entered the cave in darkness. Der. (n.) intrepidity, intrepidness; (adv.) intrepidly.

intricate - (adj.) very detailed or complicated. e.g. - Advanced mathematics involves many <u>intricate</u> theories and calculations. Der. (adv.) intricately.

intrigue - (n.) a secret plan or scheme. e.g. - The political <u>intrigue</u> involved a plan to spy on enemy governments. Der. (v.) intrigue; (adj.) intriguing; (adv.) intriguingly.

inundate - (v.) to overwhelm or overpower. e.g. - The area was <u>inundated</u> with rain in the thunderstorm last night. Der. (n.) inundation.

invigorate - (v.) to provide energy; to stimulate. e.g. - Jogging in the fresh air always <u>invigorates</u> me. Der. (n.) invigoration; (adj.) invigorating; (adj.) invigorated.

irrevocable - (adj.) impossible to be changed, altered, or taken away. e.g. - Once you sign this agreement, it is <u>irrevocable</u> and cannot be changed in any way. Der. (adv.) irrevocably; (ant.) revocable.

It doesn't hold water - (id.) it's not believable. e.g. - I don't believe him. His story <u>doesn't hold water</u>.

It was a hit - (id.) it was very popular or a huge success. e.g. - The rock group's new song <u>was a hit</u>.

It was a piece of cake - (id.) it was very easy. e.g. - The exam <u>was a piece of cake</u>. I'm sure I passed.

Exercises – I

Instructions: Complete the sentences below, using one of the words beginning with the letter "I" from the previous section. Note that some gaps require a single word, while others may need a phrasal verb or idiomatic expression. You may also need to change the form of the word. The answers are provided at the end of book.

1) Her tablecloth is always _____. There is never any spot or stain.

2) She was _____ in the robbery because she had some of the stolen money in her bag.

3) The business was _____ for two years and finally had to close down.

4) She has been an _____ of the city of Birmingham for ten years.

5) Her English is _____. Her vocabulary is precise, and her grammar is always correct.

6) The political leader _____ a rebellion against the government.

7) He is always _____. He is lazy and never gets anything done.

8) The teacher _____ the students to pay attention in class.

9) Magellan was an _____ explorer. He travelled to many parts of the world without having a rest or taking a break.

10) Working hard will have a positive _____ on your future career.

Words J to L

Instructions: Study the words below, paying attention to their meanings as well as how they are used in the example sentences. Then complete the exercise that follows.

jagged - (adj.) consisting of cut or broken edges. e.g. - The attacker threatened to cut his victim with the jagged edge of a broken bottle. Der. (n.) jaggedness; (adv.) jaggedly.

jeer - (v.) to tease or taunt; to subject to ridicule. e.g. - The cruel children jeered at the overweight boy, calling him "fatty." Der. (n.) jeer; (adj.) jeering; (adv.) jeeringly.

jeopardize - (v.) to risk or endanger. e.g. - You will jeopardize your health if you continue smoking so much. Der. (n.) jeopardy.

jot down - (id.) to write quickly in note form. e.g. - He jotted down the number that his friend gave him over the telephone.

jumbled - (adj.) disorderly or disorganized state; (syn.) cluttered. e.g. - The child's toys were laying in a jumbled pile in the corner of the room. Der. (n.) jumble; (v.) jumble.

jurisdiction - (n.) the authority to administer and apply laws and regulations. e.g. - The local sheriff has jurisdiction over this town.

keep in touch - (id.) to stay in contact with someone through telephone calls or correspondence. e.g. - Although my best friend lives miles away, we still manage to keep in touch.

Keep it down! - (id.) Be quiet! e.g. - Keep it down in there! I'm trying to study!

keep sbdy posted - (id.) to keep someone informed. e.g. - We expect to hear some news next week, so we'll keep you posted.

keep the lid on it - (id.) to keep something under control. e.g. – Inflation will continue to increase unless the government can keep the lid on it.

kernel - (1)(n.) a single seed from an ear of corn; (2)(met.) the basic or essential part. e.g. - (1) Kernels of corn are heated in oil to make popcorn; (2) The kernel of his argument was that I was lying.

kettle - (n.) a large metal container used for boiling water. e.g. - The water was boiling in the kettle.

knack - (n.) talent. e.g. - He has a knack for playing the guitar.

label - (n.) a piece of paper or plastic placed on an item for purposes of identifying its contents. e.g. - The label on the suitcase gave the name and address of its owner. Der. (v.) label.

lag - (v.) to become delayed or fall behind. e.g. - The race was close at the beginning, but the first runner won when the second runner lagged behind.

land - (v.) to find or locate. e.g. - You should be able to <u>land</u> a job. There are hundreds of employment opportunities listed in the newspaper advertisements.

lark - (n.) something done impulsively for fun or amusement. e.g. - We suddenly decided to go to the movies on a <u>lark</u>. Der. (ph. v.) lark about.

lash - (v.) to strike or hit, esp. with a whip or stick. e.g. - Slaves were often <u>lashed</u> with whips by their masters. This often caused their skin to become red or to bleed. Der. (n.) lash.

lassitude - (n.) tiredness; exhaustion. e.g. - The marathon runner showed great <u>lassitude</u> after finishing the race and rested on the grass nearby.

latent - (adj.) hidden; not obvious or visible. e.g. - The refrigerator had a <u>latent</u> defect that could not be discovered, even through careful examination. Der. (adv.) latently; (ant.) patent.

laud - (n.) praise; honour. e.g. He graduated at the top of his class and received <u>laud</u> on graduation day. Der. (v.) laud; (adj.) laudable; (adv.) laudably.

layperson - (n.) an individual possessing common knowledge on a certain subject; non-professional; non-expert. e.g. - He is a <u>layperson</u> on the subject of computers. He has no education or qualifications in that area.

ledge - (n.) a narrow shelf which sticks out from a wall of building. e.g. - Many birds were sitting outside on the high <u>ledge</u> of the building.

lenient - (adj.) easy-going about or accepting of the improper behaviour of another person. e.g. - Mary's mother is so <u>lenient</u>. She lets her do whatever she wants. Der. (n.) lenience.

let it slip - (id.) to divulge secret information. e.g. - That was supposed to be a secret, but he <u>let it slip</u>.

let the cat out of the bag - (id.) to divulge secret information. e.g. - I told her not to tell anyone, but she <u>let the cat out of the bag</u>.

liability - (n.) responsibility or obligation according to the law. e.g. - Debts which are owed to others are considered <u>liabilities</u>. Der. (adj.) liable.

licentious - (adj.) offensive in content or lacking in morality; (syn.) vulgar; lewd. e.g. - Movies with <u>licentious</u> subjects may only be seen by adults. Due to their sexual content, these films may not be seen by children.

lighten up - (id.) to relax. e.g. - You'd better learn to <u>lighten up</u> or you'll have a heart attack.

like looking for a needle in a haystack - (id.) to search for something that has many possible locations. e.g. - Searching for our lost keys on the beach was <u>like looking for a needle in a haystack</u>.

limb - (n.) an arm or leg of a human being. e.g. - You'll risk life and <u>limb</u> if you attempt to cross that busy street during rush hour.

limp - (n.) to walk unevenly, favouring one leg over another. e.g. - Pedro's broken leg did not heal properly, and he now walks with a <u>limp</u>. Der. (v.) limp.

linger - (v.) to remain or delay departure. e.g. - Fatima <u>lingered</u> at my house, talking until 2:00 a.m., although she intended to have left earlier.

livelihood - (n.) method of providing financial support for an individual's existence. e.g. - He makes his <u>livelihood</u> by working as a clerk in a grocery store.

livestock - (n.) animals which are raised for sale. e.g. - The <u>livestock</u> raised on many farms consists of cows and pigs.

livid - (adj.) angry or furious. e.g. - He was <u>livid</u> when I told him he was stupid and lazy. Der. (n.) lividity.

loathe - (v.) to hate or despise. e.g. - I <u>loathe</u> waking up early in the morning. I really can't stand it. Der. (n.) loathing; (adj.) loath, loathsome.

loiter - (v.) to remain in a place without any obvious purpose. e.g.- The youngsters were just <u>loitering</u> at the shopping centre. They had no real interest in buying anything.

loot - (v.) to seize objects during a robbery or war; (syn.) pillage, plunder. e.g. - The thieves <u>looted</u> the store, taking TVs, stereos, and microwave ovens. Der. (n.) loot; (adj.) looted.

loquacious - (adj.) eloquent or excessive in speech. e.g. - The <u>loquacious</u> speaker gave a two-hour speech at the graduation ceremony. Der. (n.) loquacity; (adv.) loquaciously.

lousy - (adj.) very poor; miserable. e.g. - I feel <u>lousy</u> today. I think I'm going to be sick.

lucrative - (adj.) relating to the production of great wealth or profit. e.g. - He was able to retire early as a result of the large sum of money he had made from <u>lucrative</u> investments. Der. (adv.) lucratively.

lukewarm - (adj.) being neither hot nor cold; (syn.) tepid. e.g. - I like to bathe in <u>lukewarm</u> water in order not to feel too hot or too cold.

lunatic - (n.) a crazy person. e.g. - He is acting like a <u>lunatic</u> lately. I think he's gone crazy. Der. (n.) lunacy.

lurch - (v.) to suddenly change course or direction. e.g. - The car suddenly <u>lurched</u> off the road and crashed into a tree.

lure - (v.) to attract or entice. e.g. - He was <u>lured</u> into buying the car by its low price. Der. (n.) lure.

lurk - (v.) to wait secretly in a place for the purpose of doing harm. e.g. - The criminal was <u>lurking</u> in the shadows, waiting to rob the old lady.

lush - (adj.) abundant in grass and greenery. e.g. - The beautiful, <u>lush</u> garden had plentiful grass and flowers. Der. (n.) lushness; (adv.) lushly.

luxurious - (adj.) providing an expensive and rich environment, beyond what is necessary. e.g. - The king lived a <u>luxurious</u> lifestyle in a palace decorated with gold. Der. (n.) luxury; (adv.) luxuriously.

Exercises – J to L

Instructions: Complete the sentences below, using one of the words beginning with the letters "J" to "L" from the previous section. Note that some gaps require a single word, while others may need a phrasal verb or idiomatic expression. You may also need to change the form of the word. The answers are provided at the end of book.

1) He _____ the address using a pen and paper.

2) The cause of certain health conditions is sometimes _____ and cannot be discovered through examinations or tests.

3) The _____ speaker gave a presentation that lasted for ninety minutes.

4) She has a _____ for music. She can sing and play the piano.

5) The clothes were in a _____ on top of the bed. She need to fold them and put them away.

6) The _____ on the package stated the nutritional information.

7) The billionaire had a _____ home that had thirty-five rooms.

8) Businesses have many _____ and other debts to be paid.

9) That magazine is _____. It may only be seen by adults.

10) The judge has _____ over the proceedings in the case.

Words – M to O

Instructions: Study the words below, paying attention to their meanings as well as how they are used in the example sentences. Then complete the exercise that follows.

magnanimity - (n.) generosity. e.g. - The wealthy family showed great <u>magnanimity</u> in donating such a large sum of money to charity. Der. (adj.) magnanimous; (adv.) magnanimously.

magnify - (v.) to make larger. e.g. – My grandmother's vision is quite bad. She can read the newspaper only with a special glass that <u>magnifies</u> the letters. Der. (n.) magnification; (adj.) magnifying.

make heads or tails of sthg - (id.) to attempt to understand something with difficulty. e.g. - I can't <u>make heads or tails of</u> this map. Do you know which road to take?

make the grade - (id.) to have an acceptable standard of performance. e.g. - I didn't get to play in the game because I couldn't <u>make the grade</u>.

make yourself scarce - (id.) to avoid friends because of a situation which has caused conflict. e.g. - I haven't seen Jodi in weeks. She has <u>made herself scarce</u>.

malice - (n.) the desire to inflict harm, esp. when caused by feelings of hatred. e.g. - The victims feel great <u>malice</u> towards their attacker and hope that he receives the death penalty. Der. (adj.) malicious; (adv.) maliciously.

mandatory - (adj.) required; necessary; obligatory; (syn.) compulsory. e.g. - Completion of this form is <u>mandatory</u>. It must be filled in by every applicant.

manifest - (v.) to show or display obviously. e.g. - The disease <u>manifests</u> itself as fever and weakness. Der. (n.) manifestation; (adv.) manifestly.

manifold - (adj.) consisting of a wide variety; many. e.g. - She had <u>manifold</u> reasons for resigning from work, including personal, professional, and health-related problems.

marginal - (adj.) very small or minimal in amount; nearly unacceptable in performance. e.g. - The company will have to close down if its profits continue to be only <u>marginal</u>. Der. (n.) margin; (adv.) marginally.

materialize - (v.) to appear or come into existence or reality. e.g. - Her dream of becoming a dancer failed to <u>materialize</u> when she was paralyzed in the accident. Der. (n.) materialization.

menace - (n.) threat or danger. e.g. - Drugs and guns are a <u>menace</u> to the well-being of today's youth. Der. (v.) menace; (adj.) menacing; (adv.) menacingly.

mettle - (n.) strength of character; courage. e.g. - The paramedic displayed great <u>mettle</u> in rescuing the man from the burning car.

migrate - (v.) to leave one climate for another for the purpose of breeding or feeding. e.g. – Certain birds <u>migrate</u> south during the winter in order to find food in warmer climates. Der. (n.) migration; (adj.) migrating.

militia - (n.) a group of individuals organized for the purpose of military service. e.g. - The militia carried out many exercises in order to prepare for war.

mischievous - (adj.) causing trouble or annoyance. e.g. - The teacher sent the mischievous pupil to the principal's office. Der. (n.) mischief; (adv.) mischievously.

misconstrue - (v.) to misunderstand. e.g. - You have completely misconstrued what I said. When I said you looked beautiful today, I didn't mean that you usually look ugly. Der. (adj.) misconstruable.

misgiving - (n.) doubt; uncertainty. e.g. - She had misgivings about marrying him when she discovered that he had a prison record.

mitigate - (v.) to lessen the severity of; (syn.) extenuate. e.g. - Your apology does not mitigate the seriousness of your mistake. Der. (n.) mitigation; (adj.) mitigating; (adj.) mitigated (ant.) unmitigated.

momentous - (adj.) notable; significant; important. e.g. - Her wedding day was one of the most momentous events of her life.

monetary - (adj.) relating to money, finance, or the economy. e.g. - The study of economics involves many monetary theories.

morsel - (n.) a small portion of food. e.g. - A morsel of food is not going to satisfy his appetite.

mouth off - (id.) to be rude or impudent. e.g. - You should be punished for mouthing off to your parents.

munch - (v.) to make a noise from the mouth while eating. e.g. - I hate the way you munch your food. Can't you eat more quietly?

municipal - (adj.) relating to the city. e.g. - The municipal authorities pay for the upkeep of city property. Der. (n.) municipality.

murky - (adj.) dark; unclear. e.g. - The water in the lake was murky. The bottom of the lake could not be seen. Der. (n.) murk, murkiness; (adv.) murkily.

neutral - (adj.) lacking in colour. e.g. - Their living room has a neutral colour scheme and is predominantly beige and white. Der. (adv.) neutrally.

nibble - (v.) to eat with very small bites. e.g. - By the way you are nibbling at your food, I take it that you're not very hungry. Der. (n.) nibble.

nitpick - (id.) to be overly concerned with very small details. e.g. - My boss is very demanding and nitpicks the smallest details.

nitwit - (id.) an idiot; a stupid person. e.g. - If you don't know that two and two equals four, you are a bigger nitwit than I thought.

no "if's", "and's" or "but's" - (id.) no excuses will be accepted. e.g. - You will do your homework. <u>No "if's", "and's" or "but's"</u>!

nominate - (v.) to select a candidate for a particular duty, esp. for public office. e.g. - The class <u>nominated</u> Abdul as their class president in the school election. Der. (n.) nomination.

notion - idea, theory, or belief. e.g. - Where did you get the crazy <u>notion</u> that the moon is made of cheese?

notorious - (adj.) relating to fame for despicable or blameworthy events or crimes. e.g. - He is <u>notorious</u> for having committed bank robbery, so everyone recognizes him. Der. (n.) notoriety; (adv.) notoriously.

noxious - (adj.) the quality of possessing a poisonous or deadly gas. e.g. - Gasoline is a <u>noxious</u> substance. Breathing excessive quantities of it can cause death. Der. (n.) noxiousness; (adv.) noxiously.

obliterate - (v.) to wipe out or destroy. e.g. - Many people fear that the world may be <u>obliterated</u> by nuclear war. Der. (n.) obliteration.

obsequious - (adj.) behaving like a servant; servile; obedient. e.g. - The waitress was <u>obsequious</u> towards the demanding customer and brought him whatever he asked for. Der. (adv.) obsequiously.

obsession - (n.) a continuing mental preoccupation with a single thought or idea which is often unreasonable or illogical. e.g. - He continued his <u>obsession</u> with finding a cure for his disease long after the doctor had told him that treatment was impossible. Der. (adj.) obsessive.

obsolete - (adj.) relating to things which are no longer useful as a result of being replaced or becoming outdated. e.g. - Computers become <u>obsolete</u> quickly nowadays as they are constantly being replaced by newer models. Der. (n.) obsolescence.

obstacle - (n.) something which holds back, delays, or prevents progress; impediment; (syn.) hindrance, stumbling block, barrier. e.g. - Despite the <u>obstacle</u> of being deaf, Beethoven was able to compose his final symphonies.

obstinacy - (n.) the action of being rigid in opinion; stubbornness. e.g. - He has displayed great <u>obstinacy</u> on this subject. I don't think that he's going to change his mind. Der. (adj.) obstinate; (adv.) obstinately.

odious - (adj.) deserving of hate; (syn.) despicable. e.g. - He was convicted of the <u>odious</u> crime of murdering small children.

on schedule - (id.) to be on time. e.g. - The bus is <u>on schedule</u> today. We should get to work on time.

once in a blue moon - (id.) something that happens very rarely. e.g. - I don't like bowling, so I do it only <u>once in a blue moon</u>.

opponent - (n.) enemy; antagonist; (syn.) adversary. e.g. - They are hardly friends. In fact, they are bitter <u>opponents</u>.

orchard - (n.) a group of fruit, nut, or olive trees; (syn.) grove. e.g. - The farm has an <u>orchard</u> containing apple and pear trees.

ordeal - (n.) a difficult or trying experience. e.g. - Cancer patients undergoing chemotherapy must endure a difficult <u>ordeal</u>.

ornate - (adj.) heavily or ostentatiously decorated. e.g. - The <u>ornate</u> castle was decorated with gold and silver, as well as priceless rugs and paintings. Der. (n.) ornateness; (adv.) ornately.

ostensibly - (adv.) in appearance. e.g. - <u>Ostensibly</u> John is a nice guy, but when you get to know him, you realize that he isn't. Der. (adj.) ostensible.

ostentatious - (adj.) relating to an obvious display, esp. of wealth. e.g. - It was very <u>ostentatious</u> of Elizabeth to wear such expensive jewellery to a charity event. Der. (adv.) ostentatiously.

out of the question - (id.) something that is impossible even to consider. e.g. - Going on vacation this year is <u>out of the question</u>. We just don't have enough money.

ovation - (n.) applause. e.g. - The singer received a standing <u>ovation</u> after his performance. Nothing could be heard over the sound of the applause.

overabundance - (n.) a huge or plentiful amount. e.g. - An <u>overabundance</u> of rain can result in flooding.

overstay one's welcome - (id.) to stay longer than one is welcome; to begin to impose upon one's host. e.g. - It was obvious that we had <u>overstayed our welcome</u> when she asked us if we would leave her house as soon as possible.

overtone - (n.) suggestion or implication; hidden meaning. e.g. - I don't like what you are implying. The <u>overtone</u> is that I'm fat and stupid.

overwhelm - (v.) to overcome or take control of an individual's thoughts, feelings, or actions. e.g. - He was <u>overwhelmed</u> with sadness when his wife died.

Exercises – M to O

Instructions: Complete the sentences below, using one of the words beginning with the letters "M" to "O" from the previous section. Note that some gaps require a single word, while others may need a phrasal verb or idiomatic expression. You may also need to change the form of the word. The answers are provided at the end of book.

1) The houses in that town were _____ by the tornado.

2) The political party _____ their candidate in the election.

3) She is so _____. I have never met anyone so stubborn.

4) He got fat due to eating an _____ of food.

5) She complains and _____ about the smallest and most insignificant things.

6) The large amount of donations given to charity during times of natural disaster shows the _____ of the general public.

7) Those chemicals are _____. You can die if you consume even small quantities of them.

8) Taking the foundation course is _____. Every student has to take it.

9) His tastes are very _____, and he likes to show off his wealth.

10) The mother's grief and rage about the murder of her daughter _____ her attack on the killer.

Words – P

Instructions: Study the words below, paying attention to their meanings as well as how they are used in the example sentences. Then complete the exercise that follows.

paramount - (adj.) highly important or significant. e.g. - If you want to get good grades, studying is <u>paramount</u>.

parsimonious - (adj.) exhibiting excessive or extreme care about money and spending. e.g. - The <u>parsimonious</u> man used his tea bags twice in order to save money. Der. (n.) parsimony; (adv.) parsimoniously.

partake - (v.) to take part in an activity with others; to participate. e.g. - Suki could not <u>partake</u> in the basketball game because she had just broken her leg.

patent - (adj.) obvious; not hidden; visible. e.g. - The television had a <u>patent</u> defect. The crack in the screen was clearly visible. Der. (adv.) patently; (ant.) latent.

patriotism - (n.) the love for or loyalty to an individual's country of nationality or citizenship. e.g. - Feelings of <u>patriotism</u> were high when the royal wedding took place. Der. (n.) patriot.

patronize - (v.) to act as a regular customer; to provide economic support. e.g. - He regularly <u>patronizes</u> the restaurant on the corner. He eats there five times a week.

peak - (n.) the highest point. e.g. - There is a great view of the city from the <u>peak</u> of that mountain. Der. (v.) peak; (adj.) peaked.

peculiar - (adj.) strange; weird. e.g. - Rosa looked really peculiar in her strange clothes and heavy make-up. Der. (n.) peculiarity; (adv.) peculiarly.

peeling - (n.) the skin of a fruit or vegetable. e.g. - The <u>peeling</u> of a banana must be removed before it can be eaten. Der. (v.) peel.

penchant - (n.) desire or preference. e.g. - Cheng is reckless and has a <u>penchant</u> for participating in dangerous activities.

penetrate - (v.) to enter inside, esp. with force. e.g. - The police <u>penetrated</u> the house where the criminals were hiding by breaking down the front door. Der. (n.) penetration; (adj.) penetrative, penetrable; penetrating; (adv.) penetratingly.

penitence - (n.) the feeling of deep regret or sorrow about one's wrongdoings; (syn.) remorse, contrition. e.g. - The murderer feels deep <u>penitence</u> for his crimes and made a full public apology to the victims' families. Der. (adj.) penitential.

perceptible - (adj.) capable of being understood by the senses. e.g. - There has been a very <u>perceptible</u> change in Nadira's behaviour. She used to be quite shy, but now is outspoken. Der. (n.) perception; (v.) perceive; (adv.) perceptibly.

perfidy - (n.) disloyalty or treason toward an individual's country of national origin. e.g. - The spy was guilty of <u>perfidy</u> because he told military secrets to other countries.

perjury - (n.) the action of lying while giving a sworn statement in court. e.g. - The witness committed <u>perjury</u> by saying that the suspect was with her at the time of the crime, although he was not. Der. (v.) perjure.

perpetually - (adv.) continuously. e.g. - I have never seen anyone as talkative as her. She talks <u>perpetually</u>. Der. (n.) perpetuation; (v.) perpetuate; (adj.) perpetual.

perturb - (v.) to cause disorder or annoyance. e.g. - The little girl's tantrum greatly <u>perturbed</u> her mother. Der. (n.) perturbation; (adj.) perturbable.

peruse - (v.) to read sthg, esp. carefully or for specific information. e.g. - Hasin <u>perused</u> the book before deciding it was interesting enough to buy. Der. (n.) perusal.

pervasive - (adj.) affecting all parts of something. e.g.- The changes to the system are <u>pervasive</u>; therefore, the system will need to be completely redone. Der. (n.) pervasion, pervasiveness; (v.) pervade; (adv.) pervasively.

pessimism - (n.) behaviour marked by expecting the worst to happen. e.g. - Deven has had a lot of bad luck in his life so, understandably, he views his future with <u>pessimism</u>. Der. (adj.) pessimistic; (adv.) pessimistically.

phlegmatic - (adj.) calm and unemotional. e.g. - He is so <u>phlegmatic</u>. I've never seen him get nervous under pressure. Der. (adv.) phlegmatically.

phony - (adj.) false, artificial, or insincere. e.g. - Her apology was <u>phony</u>. You should have known that she was being insincere.

pick a fight - (id.) to encourage a physical attack by displaying a hostile attitude. e.g. - He <u>picked a fight</u> by saying that I was too weak to hit him.

picked over - (id.) to look through carefully in order to choose the best items. e.g. – We had to <u>pick over</u> the fruit at the store because we arrived too late in the day.

pillage - (n.) the action of robbing or seizing objects, such as in a war. e.g. - The <u>pillage</u> of many shops occurred during the riot when much valuable merchandise was stolen. Der. (v.) pillage.

pin your hopes on sthg - (id.) to be very hopeful that something will happen. e.g. - I wouldn't <u>pin you hopes on</u> being accepted into medical school. You know how tough the competition is.

pinch pennies - (id.) to be very economical with money or in spending. e.g. - He is <u>pinching pennies</u> because he lost his job last month.

pioneer - (n.) an individual who goes into unexplored territory. e.g. - The <u>pioneers</u> travelled west to unsettled land. Der. (v.) pioneer; (adj.) pioneering.

pique - (v.) to irritate or provoke. e.g. - You <u>piqued</u> my curiosity by telling me that you have a surprise for me. Please tell me more.

pittance - (n.) a very small wage or amount of money. e.g. - Kazuo makes such a <u>pittance</u> at work that he can hardly feed his children.

play with fire - (id.) to become involved in a dangerous situation. e.g. - If you decide to cheat on the test, you're really <u>playing with fire</u>.

plentiful - (adj.) abundant; more than enough. e.g. - Plants cannot grow without <u>plentiful</u> sunshine. Der. (n.) plenty; (adv.) plentifully.

plot - (n.) the organization or plan of a story. e.g. - The <u>plot</u> of the story was about two twins who had been separated at birth. Der. (v.) plot.

plump - (adj.) fat; thick and round. e.g. - <u>Plump</u> tomatoes make better spaghetti sauce. Smaller ones aren't usually as tasty. Der. (v.) plump.

ponder - (v.) to think about or consider deeply. e.g. - He sat by the lake for hours <u>pondering</u> the meaning of life. Der. (adj.) ponderable.

populace - (n.) people residing in a certain area. e.g. - The <u>populace</u> of the city of Chicago is asked to limit its electricity use during the summer. Der. (n.) population; (v.) populate; (adj.) populated.

posterity - (n.) future generations; descendants. e.g. - The rich man invested his money wisely so that his <u>posterity</u> would have a large inheritance.

potential - (adj.) possible; capable of becoming fact. e.g. - Every job applicant is considered to be a <u>potential</u> employee. Der. (n.) potential; (adv.) potentially.

precarious - (adj.) dangerous; (syn.) treacherous. e.g. - His car was hanging off the side of the mountain in a <u>precarious</u> position after the accident. Der. (n.) precariousness; (adv.) precariously.

precedent - (n.) a previous event, esp. one which establishes a pattern for subsequent behaviour. e.g. - The judge sentenced the criminal to the death penalty. This set a <u>precedent</u> for the use of the death penalty for subsequent crimes. Der. (v.) precede.

precinct - (n.) territory of a city established for police control. e.g. - New York City has many police <u>precincts</u>, which are usually established according to neighbourhood boundaries.

precipitate - (v.) to cause or bring about, especially suddenly. e.g. - The violence <u>precipitated</u> full-scale war. Der. (n.) precipitation; (adj.) precipitous.

predator - (n.) an individual or animal that preys or kills. e.g. - The American black bear is a <u>predator</u> because it kills other animals and sometimes humans.

predicament - (n.) dilemma; difficult situation. e.g. - He was left in a <u>predicament</u> when his car broke down on the motorway at 4:00 a.m.

predilection - (n.) a desire or preference. e.g. - She has an overwhelming <u>predilection</u> for chocolate and always wants to eat it.

predominant - (adj.) playing a major or significant role; (syn.) prominent. e.g. - He was a predominant contributor to the hospital building fund, donating over £1,000,000. Der. (n.) predomination; (v.) predominate; (adv.) predominantly.

prematurely - (adv.) too early. e.g. - The baby was born prematurely in March. It shouldn't have been born until May. Der. (adj.) premature.

premise - (n.) an area of land which contains buildings. e.g. - Rashid is a security guard at the factory. His job is to protect the premises against theft.

prerogative - (n.) a special option, decision, or privilege. e.g. - She wasn't required to attend the lesson. On the contrary, it was her prerogative.

prevalent - (adj.) commonly practiced; continuing in use or acceptance; (syn.) widespread. e.g. - Skiing is prevalent in mountainous areas. Der. (v.) prevail; (adj.) prevalently.

pricey - (id.) very expensive. e.g. - They can eat at that pricey restaurant because they have a lot of money.

proliferation - (n.) an amount which is excessive in growth or quantity; plethora. e.g. - J.S. Bach composed a proliferation of symphonies in his lifetime. Der. (v.) proliferate; (adj.) prolific: (adv.) prolifically.

prominent - (adj.) playing a major or significant role. e.g. - Your grades in high school play a prominent role in determining which college you can attend. Der. (n.) prominence; (adv.) prominently.

prompt - (v.) to cause; to bring about a result or action. e.g. - The rainy weather prompted the cancellation of the football match.

prone (to) - (adj.) having a certain tendency or vulnerability. e.g. - Nico is clumsy and is therefore prone to accidents. Der. (n.) proneness; (adv.) pronely.

propensity - (n) a desire or preference that appears natural to a certain person. e.g. - His propensity to overeat is obvious because he is so overweight. Der. (v.) propend; (adj.) propense.

proposition - (n.) a problem put forward for consideration. e.g. - The city considered the mayor's proposition to build a new road through the city centre. Der. (v.) propose.

prosecute - (v.) to take to court for the commission of a crime. e.g. - The suspect was prosecuted in court for murder and was found not guilty. Der. (n.) prosecution.

prostrate - (adj.) lying in a face-down position; sometimes used to describe an act of worship. e.g. - The patient was lying prostrate after his heart attack and had to be turned face-up so that first aid could be administered.

protocol - (n.) standards of conduct. e.g. - Old-fashioned protocol dictated that men should always open doors for women.

protract - (v.) to continue for an extended time. e.g. - The journey was <u>protracted</u> by several delays as a result of the bad weather conditions.

provident - (adj.) the provision for unforeseen events in the future; careful; prudent. e.g. - It was very <u>provident</u> of you to bring an umbrella as rain is forecast. Der. (n.) providence.

provoke - (v.) to cause or incite anger. e.g. - Her outrageous behaviour <u>provoked</u> her father and caused him to scream and yell at her. Der. (n.) provocation; (adj.) provocative; (adv.) provocatively.

prudence - (n.) the exercise of care or caution. e.g. - You must exercise <u>prudence</u> in your investments. Otherwise, you might lose a substantial amount of money. Der. (adj.) prudent; (adv.) prudently; (ant.) imprudent.

pugnacious - (adj.) exceptionally aggressive or quarrelsome in behaviour. e.g. - Sean is so <u>pugnacious</u>. He is always trying to start arguments. Der. (adv.) pugnaciously.

pull through - (id.) to survive an accident or illness. e.g. - The doctors say that Kareem will <u>pull through</u> his accident.

punch - (v.) to hit with a closed hand. e.g. - The boxer fell to the floor when he was <u>punched</u> by his opponent. Der. (n.) punch.

purge - (v.) to dispose of, esp. with force. e.g. - The hospital attendants had to pump the child's stomach in order to <u>purge</u> the poison from his body. Der. (n.) purge.

pursuit - (n.) a hobby or undertaking. e.g. - His favourite <u>pursuits</u> include stamp collecting and playing the guitar. Der. (v.) pursue.

put yourself in my shoes - (id.) to try to understand the situation another person is in. e.g. - If you'd <u>put yourself in my shoes</u>, you would understand why I did what I had to do.

putrid - (adj.) being highly unpleasant or repugnant; rotten. e.g. - This food is <u>putrid</u> and is not fit to eat. Der. (adv.) putridly.

Exercises – P

Instructions: Complete the sentences below, using one of the words beginning with the letter "P" from the previous section. Note that some gaps require a single word, while others may need a phrasal verb or idiomatic expression. You may also need to change the form of the word. The answers are provided at the end of book.

1) She was very _____ when she spoke to the group. She didn't appear nervous at all.

2) Small villages were often _____ in the Middle Ages as attackers and raiders stole the possessions of the local people.

3) The _____ of the mountain is 12,000 feet above sea level.

4) He was a _____ in the field of bio-engineering. In fact, he was the first scientist to devote himself to research in the area.

5) The child was lying in a _____ position after the accident.

6) That cheese is _____. You will get sick if you eat it.

7) She is _____ if she is thinking about lying to her parents.

8) The completion of the project was _____ by several months because of a lack of financing.

9) There has been a _____ shift in the attitude of the class after the teacher told us off. Some students used to disrespect the teacher, but they don't anymore.

10) The specialist said she would _____ her cancer treatment and make a full recovery.

Words – Q to R

Instructions: Study the words below, paying attention to their meanings as well as how they are used in the example sentences. Then complete the exercise that follows.

quaint - (adj.) charming and old-fashioned. e.g. - The old-fashioned Austrian village had a quaint atmosphere.

quarters - (n.) accommodation, usually for soldiers or animals. e.g. - Soldiers on the army base sleep in shared quarters containing twelve beds.

quarry - (n.) an open area from which rock, such as marble, is removed. e.g. - The workers were removing rock and marble from the quarry, using heavy machinery.

querulous - (adj.) characterized by constant complaining. e.g. - The man became querulous in old age and began to complain about everything. Der. (n.) querulousness; (adv.) querulously.

quest - (n.) a mission or adventure in pursuit of a specific purpose. e.g. - The doctors went on a quest to the African jungle to find rare plants to use in the manufacture of medicine.

quirk - (n.) unnatural behaviour or affectation; idiosyncrasy. e.g. - Jodi has the strange quirk of checking her alarm clock ten times before going to bed. Der. (n.) quirkiness; (adj.) quirky; (adv.) quirkily.

racy - (adj.) sexually suggestive or sensational. e.g. - The actress wore a racy dress which was very low-cut in the front.

radical - (adj.) extreme; non-conservative; non-traditional. e.g. - He has radical political theories. In fact, he believes that the government should be abolished entirely. Der. (adv.) radically.

rancid - (adj.) having a bad smell or taste. e.g. - You had better not eat that food. It is rancid. Der. (n.) rancidity, rancidness; (adv.) rancidly.

ransack - (v.) to throw into disorder or disorganization as a result of searching for valuables, esp. during a burglary. e.g. - The burglars ransacked the house in search of jewellery and money. Der. (adj.) ransacked.

ransom - (1)(n.) the rescue from captivity by paying money; (2)(met.) release from punishment. e.g. - (1) The kidnapping victim was released after the ransom was paid. (2) Many religions believe in ransom for the punishment for sins.

rapt - (adj.) totally attracted to; (syn.) enchanted. e.g. - The children were giving their rapt attention to the TV program and didn't hear their mother calling them to dinner. Der. (v.) enrapture.

ravine - (n.) a small valley with steep sides. e.g. - A ravine had been formed in the field where a small fresh-water spring used to flow.

reap - (v.)(met.) to win, acquire, or attain. e.g. - After years of hard work, he finally <u>reaped</u> some benefit from his efforts.

receptacle - (n.) a container used for collecting items which are later thrown away. e.g. - All litter should be thrown into the <u>receptacles</u> provided throughout the park.

recess - (v.) to interrupt or suspend an activity or procedure. e.g. - The children are not in class right now. They have <u>recessed</u> for lunch. Der. (n.) recess.

recession - (1)(n.) a group which leaves at the end of a ceremony; (2)(n.) a decline in the general economy. e.g. - (1) It took the funeral <u>recession</u> half an hour to cross the road since thousands of people had attended. (2) Jobs are difficult to find during an economic <u>recession</u>. Der. (v.) recede.

recite - (v.) to say or repeat a script from memory. e.g. - All students will be expected to memorize the poem and <u>recite</u> it to the class before the end of the term. Der. (n.) recital, recitation; (adj.) recited.

recover with flying colours - (id.) to recover very well after an accident or injury. e.g. - Husna is <u>recovering with flying colours</u> after her operation and should be out of the hospital by the weekend.

recruitment - (n.) the process of adding new individuals to activities of employment. e.g. - He works for an employment agency. His job is the <u>recruitment</u> of new managers for employment with various companies. Der. (v.) recruit.

rectify - (v.) to make right or correct. e.g. - The bank has promised to <u>rectify</u> the error they made on my account. Der. (n.) rectification; (adj.) rectified.

recuperate - (v.) to recover health after an extended illness or operation; (syn.) convalesce. e.g. - He is in bed <u>recuperating</u> after suffering another heart attack. Der. (n.) recuperation.

red tape - (id.) complications or paperwork involved in government procedures or bureaucracy. e.g. - Applying for a job with the government involves a lot of <u>red tape</u>.

refectory - (n.) a place for eating and drinking. e.g. - The students were gathered in the <u>refectory</u>, eating their lunch.

refinement - (n.) the action of improving or perfecting. e.g. - Petroleum oil must go through <u>refinement</u> before it can be used as gasoline. Der. (v.) refine; (adj.) refined.

refrain (from) - (v.) to restrain or prevent oneself from doing something. e.g. - The hospital is a smoke-free zone. That means you must <u>refrain</u> from smoking.

regime - (n.) a strict form of management or government. e.g. - Fang has a strict exercise <u>regime</u>. She goes to the gym every day.

register - (v.) to officially record an individual's name in a book or list. e.g. - Daksha <u>registered</u> for classes at the university last week. Der. (n.) registration.

regress - (v.) to return to an earlier time period. e.g. - Being overwhelmed by the responsibilities of adult life, Haru wished that she could <u>regress</u> to her childhood. Der. (n.) regression.

rehabilitation - (n.) the action of returning to a state of good health, esp. through the use of therapy. e.g. - After years of alcoholism, Lindsay is finally undergoing <u>rehabilitation</u> in order to stop drinking. Der. (v.) rehabilitate; (adj.) rehabilitated.

rehearsal - (n.) a preparatory performance or recital. e.g. - The orchestra had several <u>rehearsals</u> before they held a concert for the public. Der. (v.) rehearse; (adj.) rehearsed.

reiterate - (v.) to repeat or emphasize again. e.g. - The teacher <u>reiterated</u> the instructions to the examination after the student asked a question about them. Der. (n.) reiteration; (adj.) reiterative; (adv.) reiteratively.

relapse - (n.) the action of returning to a previous condition, esp. for the worse; deterioration. e.g. - Kendra had not used drugs for years, but she had a <u>relapse</u> last weekend. Der. (v.) relapse.

relegate - (v.) to assign to an inferior group or category. e.g. - The football player was <u>relegated</u> another league when he began to play poorly. Der. (n.) relegation.

relic - (n.) an item of historical or archaeological significance. e.g. - The Museum of Natural History contains many archaeological <u>relics</u>, many of which are over 2,000 years old.

relinquish - (v.) to surrender or give up. e.g. - The single mother was forced to <u>relinquish</u> her children to the state when she was sentenced to prison. Der. (n.) relinquishment.

relish - (v.) to enjoy very much. e.g. - I <u>relish</u> long walks in the open air during the summer.

reluctant - (adj.) hesitant or unready to act. e.g. - Deepal was <u>reluctant</u> to accept the job when she heard that the salary was quite low. Der. (n.) reluctance; (adv.) reluctantly.

remedy - (n.) a cure or therapy. e.g. - A common <u>remedy</u> for headache is aspirin. Der. (v.) remedy; (adj.) remedial.

remorse - (n.) the feeling of guilt or sadness about one's own wrongdoings; (syn.) penitence, contrition. e.g. - The murderer showed great <u>remorse</u> for his crimes and asked for the forgiveness of the public. Der. (adj.) remorseful; (adv.) remorsefully.

remunerate - (v.) to pay for a service performed; compensate. e.g. - The company agreed to <u>remunerate</u> me quite highly. My salary will be $20,000 a month. Der. (n.) remuneration; (adj.) remunerated.

render - (v.) to give or provide, esp. a service. e.g. - You must pay the applicable fee for any services <u>rendered</u> to you.

renounce - (v.) to refuse to obey or recognize the authority of. e.g. - Many people who <u>renounced</u> Hitler during World War II were put to death Der. (n.) renouncement.

renovate - (v.) to renew; to improve the condition of. e.g. - That hotel is currently being <u>renovated</u>. They are repairing the damage caused by the fire. Der. (n.) renovation; (adj.) renovated.

repel - (v.) to push back or away. e.g. - This spray <u>repels</u> mosquitoes because the smell is offensive to them. Der. (n.) repulsion, repellent; (adj.) repulsive.

repent - (v.) to ask forgiveness for a sin or wrongdoing. e.g. - I forgave her after she sincerely <u>repented</u> and apologized. Der. (n.) repentance.

replete (with) - (adj.) complete; abundant. e.g. - The orchestra was <u>replete</u> with all types of wind and string instruments. Der. (n.) repleteness, repletion.

reprehensible - (adj.) suitable of receiving great blame or criticism; (syn.) culpable. e.g. - Committing murder is a <u>reprehensible</u> act. Der. (n.) reprehension, reprehensibility; (v.) reprehend; (adv.) reprehensibly.

reproach - (v.) to give severe criticism or blame. e.g. - The mother <u>reproached</u> her child for spilling the milk. Der. (n.) reproach; (adj.) reproachful; (adv.) reproachfully; (exp.) beyond reproach.

reproduce - (v.) to prepare a copy of something from its original source. e.g. - The secretary <u>reproduced</u> the contract by making a photocopy. Der. (n.) reproduction; (adj.) reproduced.

residue - (n.) part of something which is left over after the main part has been taken away. e.g. - I hate this soap. It leaves a strange <u>residue</u> on my skin that can't be rinsed off. Der. (adj.) residual; (adv.) residually.

resign yourself to a situation - (id.) to accept a bad situation and stop attempting to change it for the better. e.g. - Bettina used to hate living with her mother-in-law, but has finally <u>resigned herself to the situation</u>.

resolute - (adj.) acting decisively and with determination. e.g. - He was <u>resolute</u> in his decision to attend college. In fact, he said that nothing could change his mind. Der. (n.) resolve; (v.) resolve; (adv.) resolutely.

respiration - (n.) the action of breathing. e.g. - <u>Respiration</u> and heart beat must be present in order for an individual to remain alive after an accident. Der. (v.) respire.

reticent - (adj.) reluctant or unwilling to talk. e.g. - The suspect was <u>reticent</u> when asked about his participation in the crime.

retire - (v.) to go to bed. e.g. - I feel tired and would like to <u>retire</u> for the evening.

retract - (v.) to draw back; to withdraw. e.g. - The newspaper <u>retracted</u> the false information that it gave in the article and offered a full apology.

retreat - (n.) a private place, often used to spend time alone. e.g. - Kiku's husband is away for the weekend on a <u>retreat</u> in the mountains. Der. (v.) retreat.

retrieve - (v.) to get or bring back again. e.g. - The information could not be <u>retrieved</u> from the computer system. It must not have been stored properly in the memory. Der. (n.) retrieval; (adj.) retrievable.

retrospect - (n.) the examination of an event after it has occurred. e.g. - In <u>retrospect</u>, he realizes that it was a mistake to have taken the job. Der. (adj.) retrospective; (adv.) retrospectively.

revel - (v.) to celebrate, esp. wildly. e.g. - They <u>revelled</u> all night at the party and were still drunk in the morning. Der. (n.) revelry.

revile - (v.) to criticize severely; scold; chide; rebuke; (syn.) reproach. e.g. - The newspaper article <u>reviled</u> the government for not providing adequate funding for educational programs.

ring a bell - (id.) to sound familiar. e.g. - Now that you mention it, that story does <u>ring a bell</u>.

ringleader - (n.) leader of a group that participates in illegal activities. e.g. - The <u>ringleader</u> of the gang is thought to have organized the sale of narcotic drugs.

rivalry - (n.) competition; opposition. e.g. - The two opposing teams engage in a friendly <u>rivalry</u>. Der. (n.) rival; (v.) rival.

rodent - (n.) a small unwanted animal, such as a rat or a mouse. e.g. - You can set a trap or use poison to deal with <u>rodents</u> in your home.

roomy - (adj.) having enough space or room; (syn.) spacious. e.g. - The hotel was quite <u>roomy</u> and could accommodate 2,000 guests. Der. (n.) roominess.

rudimentary - (adj.) basic or fundamental. e.g. - You will never understand advanced mathematics if you don't learn the <u>rudimentary</u> principles of arithmetic. Der. (n.) rudiment; (adv.) rudimentarily.

rummage - (v.) to cause disorder while searching for something. e.g. - We <u>rummaged</u> through the attic looking for old photographs. Der. (adj.) rummage.

ruthless - (adj.) cruel; malicious. e.g. - He is known for especially <u>ruthless</u> crimes against the elderly. Der. (n.) ruthlessness; (adv.) ruthlessly.

Exercises – Q to R

Instructions: Complete the sentences below, using one of the words beginning with the letters "Q" or "R" from the previous section. Note that some gaps require a single word, while others may need a phrasal verb or idiomatic expression. You may also need to change the form of the word. The answers are provided at the end of book.

1) After years of drug addiction, she is finally undergoing _____.

2) The company will begin to _____ the service once you have paid the deposit.

3) The _____ restaurant tried to recreate the atmosphere of the 1950s.

4) You will need a few months to _____ after your back operation is done.

5) The explorer went on a _____ to India to try to find the endangered species of tigers.

6) The president had to _____ control of the company after the merger was complete.

7) The army officer's job is the _____ of new soldiers.

8) Her _____ of constantly pushing her glasses up her nose gets a bit distracting.

9) In _____, he wishes that he had gone to college after all.

10) I was _____ to lie to the police officer since I knew the punishment would be severe.

Words – S

Instructions: Study the words below, paying attention to their meanings as well as how they are used in the example sentences. Then complete the exercise that follows.

sacred - (adj.) reverent; holy; (syn.) pious. e.g. – Temples, mosques, and churches are considered <u>sacred</u> since religious worship occurs there.

sag - (v.) to lose tightness or firmness. e.g. - She doesn't look young anymore. Her skin has started to <u>sag</u> and wrinkle. Der. (n.) (adj.) sagging; (adj.) sagged.

salvage - (v.) to save something, esp. that which has been damaged. e.g. - It was possible to <u>salvage</u> the car after the accident. It is being fixed at the garage right now. Der. (n.) salvage; (adj.) salvageable.

sanctimonious - (adj.) relating to an insincere or hypocritical adherence to high moral standards. e.g. - The wealthy king gave a <u>sanctimonious</u> speech about how money should not be considered the most important thing in life. Der. (n.) sanctimony, (adv.) sanctimoniously.

saunter - (v.) to walk in an unhurried manner; (syn.) stroll. e.g. - The couple slowly <u>sauntered</u> down the street, looking in the store windows. Der. (n.) saunter.

scald - (v.) to burn with hot water. e.g. - The hot coffee spilled, <u>scalding</u> the baby's skin and causing it to turn red. Der. (adj.) scalding, scalded.

scant - (adj.) a very small amount. Due to <u>scant</u> attendance, class was cancelled. Der. (adj.) scanty; (adv.) scantily.

scarlet - (adj.) bright red. e.g. - Her face turned <u>scarlet</u> from being in the sun too long.

scathing - (adj.) harsh; severe; damaging. e.g. - The senator presented a <u>scathing</u> attack on the proposed law. Der. (n.) scathe; (v.) scathe; (adv.) scathingly.

scorch - (v.) to burn with dry heat. e.g. - He <u>scorched</u> the shirt while ironing it, leaving a huge burn on the sleeve. Der. (adj.) scorched.

scrape - (n.) an area on the body where the surface of the skin has been removed. e.g. - The child fell off his bicycle and got a <u>scrape</u> on his knee from the rough pavement. Der. (v.) scrape; (adj.) scraped.

scribbled - (adj.) written in an illegible or disorganized manner. e.g. - Can you make out this <u>scribbled</u> message? The handwriting is so unclear that I can't read it. Der. (n.) scribble; (v.) scribble.

script - (n.) a written, detailed plan, such as for a play or movie. e.g. - The actor studied the <u>script</u> in order to memorize his part.

scrumptious - (adj.) delicious; very tasty; (syn.) delectable. e.g. - This cake is <u>scrumptious</u>. I have never tasted anything so delicious.

scruples - (n.) morals; ethics; standards of behaviour. e.g. - People displaying immoral behaviour do not have the proper <u>scruples</u>. Der. (adj.) scrupulous; (adv.) scrupulously; (ant.) unscrupulous.

scrutinize - (v.) to examine in great detail. e.g. - He <u>scrutinized</u> the artwork in order to determine if it was authentic. Der. (n.) scrutiny.

seal - (n.) a stamp or symbol. e.g. - Your diploma contains the official college <u>seal</u> in the lower left-hand corner.

search high and low - (id.) to search for something extensively. e.g. - I've <u>searched high and low</u> for my car keys, but I still can't find them.

secession - (n.) the action of taking back membership or property from a group or union; withdrawal. e.g. - The <u>secession</u> of a small group of citizens reduced the town's population. Der. (v.) secede.

sect - (n.) a group observing certain religious beliefs which are often strict or fanatical. e.g. - Certain religious <u>sects</u> require their followers to have short hair and wear only simple clothing.

sedate - (v.) to make calm or quiet, esp. with the use of medication. e.g. - The doctor <u>sedated</u> the patient with tranquilizers. Der. (n.) sedation; (adj.) sedate; (adj.) sedated.

seize - (v.) to take hold of something with force or strength. e.g. - The policeman <u>seized</u> the escaped criminal by grabbing him with both arms. Der. (n.) seizure.

sentence (to) - (v.) to specify the punishment for a criminal convicted of a crime. e.g. - The attacker was <u>sentenced</u> to seven years in prison for his involvement in the assault on the elderly woman. Der. (n.) sentence.

sentry - (n.) a soldier standing guard. e.g. - A <u>sentry</u> was standing guard at the main gate of the army base.

sequence - (n.) the order or series of individual items. e.g. - The files should be organized in numerical <u>sequence</u> from one to one hundred. Der. (v.) sequence; (adj.) sequential; (adv.) sequentially.

serene - (adj.) peaceful; (syn.) placid. e.g. - They enjoyed <u>serene</u> surroundings during their vacation at an isolated cabin in the north woods. Der. (n.) serenity; (adv.) serenely.

servility - (n.) relating to the behaviour of a servant or an individual in an inferior position. e.g. - The employee responded with complete <u>servility</u>, doing whatever his boss demanded. Der. (adj.) servile; (adv.) servilely.

set sbdy straight - (id.) to point out a mistake in another person's behaviour or thinking. e.g. - I need to <u>set you straight</u>. The bus leaves at 3:00, not 3:30.

set the record straight - (id.) to provide someone with correct information after they have been misinformed. e.g. - I want to <u>set the record straight</u>. I paid £2 for the tickets, not £20.

setback - (n.) an event which causes a reversal in progress. e.g. - The poor weather conditions caused a setback to our journey, and we were delayed three hours. Der. (ph. v.) set back.

severity - (n.) seriousness. e.g. - The severity of punishment shall be equal to the seriousness of the crime. Der. (adj.) severe; (adv.) severely.

shady - (adj.) being of doubtful quality or character; dubious. e.g. - Maybe people do change, but I think he's a shady character.

shed light on sthg - (id.) to explain. e.g. - Could you shed some light on this homework?

shell - (v.) to drop bombs. e.g. - When London was heavily shelled during World War II, its residents often took shelter in subway tunnels to avoid being killed in the bombing. Der. (n.) shell.

shelter - (n.) something that provides cover and protection. e.g. - We took shelter under a tree when it started to rain. Der. (v.) shelter; (adj.) sheltered.

show sbdy the ropes - (id.) to provide someone with instructions. e.g. - He showed me the ropes on my first day of work.

skeletons in your cupboard - (id.) to hide secrets about your past. e.g. - Nina doesn't talk a lot about her past. I wonder if she has skeletons in her cupboard.

shred - (v.) to cut or tear into small pieces. e.g. - Cheese is usually shredded before it is placed on the top of pizza. Der. (n.) shredder; (adj.) shredded.

shrewd - (adj.) possessing awareness and cleverness in business dealings. e.g. - He is a very shrewd businessperson and now owns over 200 convenience stores. Der. (n.) shrewdness; (adv.) shrewdly.

shrill - (adj.) sharp; high pitched. e.g. - Your voice is very shrill. I think you are singing in the wrong key.

shrivel - (v.) to cause to become wrinkled from age or lack of moisture. My grandmother's skin shrivelled as she became older. Der. (adj.) shrivelled.

shrug - (v.) to move the shoulders upwards to show disinterest or uncertainty. e.g. - When I asked Whitney if she would go to the party, she just shrugged her shoulders and changed the subject.

simmer - (v.) to cook over a low heat. e.g. - This soup should be simmered for thirty minutes at a low temperature.

simulate - (v.) to reproduce or copy the appearance of. e.g. - The restaurant tries to simulate the atmosphere from the 1950's. Der. (n.) simulation; (adj.) simulated.

simultaneously - (adv.) at the same time. e.g. - Twins or triplets celebrate their birthdays simultaneously. Der. (n.) simultaneousness, simultaneity; (adj.) simultaneous.

sinecure - (n.) employment for which an individual is paid, but for which no duties or responsibilities are required. e.g. - Haaziq is retired now. His job as city clerk is only a <u>sinecure</u> since he doesn't actually work, but still receives a salary.

size up - (id.) to make an estimation of or decision about the value or worth of something; (syn.) evaluate. e.g. - The town's people <u>sized up</u> the damage caused by the earthquake.

skirmish - (n.) a small fight in a war. e.g. - It was not a full-scale battle, but only a small <u>skirmish</u>.

skyrocket - (v.) to rapidly increase to an excessive amount. e.g. - The early frost in Florida has caused the price of oranges to <u>skyrocket</u>.

slander - (v.) to cause damage to an individual's reputation as a result of lying, rumors, or gossip. e.g. - You should not destroy his good name through such <u>slander</u>. Der. (n.) slander.

slash - (n.) a long, narrow cut; (syn.) slit. e.g. - She bled to death from the self-inflicted <u>slashes</u> on her wrists. Der. (v.) slash.

sleek - (adj.) having a smooth, bright surface. e.g. - The new motorcycle had a <u>sleek</u> surface as a result of the bright paint that had been applied to it. Der. (n.) sleekness; (v.) sleek; (adv.) sleekly.

slippery - (adj.) the quality of causing something to fall or change position as a result of being wet or moist. e.g. - Be careful when you walk on the floor. You might fall as I have just mopped it, and it might still be <u>slippery</u>. Der. (v.) slip.

slit - (n.) a long, narrow cut; (syn.) slash. e.g. - This envelope has been opened. It has a <u>slit</u> along the side. Der. (v.) slit.

slovenly - (adj.) unclean in behaviour or appearance. e.g. - He looked <u>slovenly</u> in his dirty shoes and torn jeans.

sluggish - (adj.) slow in activity or movement. e.g. - The <u>sluggish</u> movement of the train caused its arrival to be delayed by one hour. Der. (adv.) sluggishly.

smear - (v.) to spread or rub out. e.g. - The glass was <u>smeared</u> with fingerprints and needed to be washed. Der. (n.) smear.

smother - (v.) to stop the breathing of another person by placing an object over the face, esp. a pillow. e.g. - The victim's breathing stopped when he was <u>smothered</u> with a pillow.

snag - (n.) problem or difficulty. e.g. - We experienced several <u>snags</u> on our vacation, including being robbed and losing our luggage. Der. (v.) snag.

sneaky - (adj.) relating to an individual who uses dishonesty or exploitation; sly; (syn.) cunning. e.g. - It was very <u>sneaky</u> of him to steal money from the people who had grown to trust him. Der. (n.) sneak; (v.) sneak.

snub - (v.) to shun or avoid socially. e.g. - She is a conceited woman and often <u>snubs</u> us in public when she is with her wealthy friends.

soak - (v.) to become full or covered with water or moisture; (syn.) drench. e.g. - The towel was <u>soaked</u> after we used it to wipe up the water.

sober - (adj.) being fully in control of one's faculties; not drunk. e.g. - Many accidents occur because some people are not <u>sober</u> when they drive.

solicit - (v.) to request; to attempt to acquire or obtain. e.g. - After being charged with murder, he <u>solicited</u> the advice of a lawyer. Der. (n.) solicitation.

spacious - (adj.) having enough room or space; (syn.) roomy. e.g. - Our house is quite <u>spacious</u>. It has seventeen rooms. Der. (n.) spaciousness; (adv.) spaciously.

spawn - (v.) to produce or cause to develop; to create. e.g. - His argumentative attitude often <u>spawns</u> many disagreements. Der. (n.) spawn.

specimen - (n.) a sample, esp. one used for purposes of examination. e.g. - The doctor took a blood <u>specimen</u> from my arm in order to determine the cause of my illness.

spill the beans - (id.) to divulge secret information. e.g. - She <u>spilled the beans</u> about all the confidential information that I had told her.

spine - (n.) the backbone. e.g. - He is paralyzed from the chest down as a result of an injury to the top part of his <u>spine</u>. Der. (adj.) spinal.

splinter - (n.) a small fragment of wood. e.g. - A piece of wood broke off of the table and left a <u>splinter</u> in my finger. Der. (adj.) splintered.

sponsor - (v.) to provide support or financing for a specific activity, esp. by an institution or organization. e.g. - Coca-Cola <u>sponsored</u> the Olympic Games by providing substantial financial support. Der. (n.) sponsor, sponsorship; (adj.) sponsored.

spring up - (id.) to appear quickly or unexpectedly from a specific source. e.g. - A leak suddenly <u>sprang up</u> from the water pipe.

sprout - (v.) to grow from a planted seed. e.g. - The first traces of greenery appeared through the soil as the seeds began to <u>sprout</u>. Der. (n.) sprout.

squalor - (n.) Many houses in the poor, run-down neighbourhood exist in a state of <u>squalor</u>. Der. (adj.) squalid.

squat - (v.) to stand on one's feet, low to the ground, with the knees bent; (syn.) crouch. e.g. - He was <u>squatting</u> by the fireplace, trying to start the fire.

stack - (n.) a pile of items placed in a vertical position, one on the top of the other. e.g. - Huan had a <u>stack</u> of books on his desk that was two feet high. Der. (v.) stack; (adj.) stacked.

stagnant - (adj.) not moving; standing still. e.g. - The water in this lake is <u>stagnant</u> since it doesn't flow to another waterway. Der. (n.) stagnation; (v.) stagnate; (adv.) stagnantly.

stained - (adj.) to discolour cloth materials with dirt, food, or drink. e.g. - His jeans became grass-<u>stained</u> while playing football. Der. (n.) stain; (v.) stain.

stale - (adj.) lacking in freshness or flavour. e.g. - This bread is <u>stale</u> and is too hard to eat.

staunch - (adj.) relating to strength in one's beliefs or opinions. e.g. - He is a <u>staunch</u> supporter of the Republican Party and often donates money to their campaigns. Der. (adv.) staunchly.

steer clear of - (id.) to avoid. e.g. - If you <u>steer clear of</u> the dangerous areas when you are in New York City, you shouldn't have any problem.

stench - (n.) an offensive smell or odour. e.g. - Your dirty socks are giving off a <u>stench</u>. Why don't you wash them?

sthg up your sleeve - (id.) to hide information about something. e.g. - Is that all you wanted to tell me or do you have <u>something up your sleeve</u>?

stick to your guns - (id.) not changing one's mind or opinion. e.g. - He won't change his mind because he always <u>sticks to his guns</u>.

sticky - (adj.)(1) covered with glue; adhesive. (2)(met.) a difficult or problematic situation. e.g. - (1) The adhesive tape was <u>sticky</u> on both sides. (2) He found himself in a <u>sticky</u> situation when his wife discovered that he was having an affair. Der. (n.) sticker; (v.) stick.

stifle - (v.) to suppress, discourage, or hold back. e.g. - Why do you always <u>stifle</u> me when I want to speak? I have the right to express my opinions.

stingy - (adj.) not generous with money or in spending. e.g. - He is so <u>stingy</u> that he insists on her paying whenever they go out. Der. (n.) stinginess; (adv.) stingily

stocky - (adj.) relating to men who have a short, muscular build. e.g. - Aaron is <u>stocky</u> because weight-lifting is his hobby.

stood up - (id.) to have an appointment or a date broken by someone. e.g. - I was supposed to meet Isaac at 10:00, but he <u>stood me up</u>.

stoop - (v.) to bend forward from the waist or shoulders. e.g. - The hiker <u>stooped</u> forward from the weight of his backpack.

stout - (adj.) strong and healthy. e.g. - The army captain was a <u>stout</u> man who was six feet tall and weighed 210 pounds. Der. (adv.) stoutly.

strand - (v.) to cause to be left alone, esp. in a vulnerable or dangerous situation. e.g. – Robinson Crusoe was <u>stranded</u> on a desert island and waited to be rescued. Der. (adj.) stranded.

strangle - (v.) to stop the breathing of another person by placing a rope or the hands around the neck. e.g. - The police investigation determined that the victim was <u>strangled</u> since her neck was bruised. Der. (n.) strangulation.

strapping - (adj.) very strong and healthy; (syn.) hearty. e.g. - Kerry is a <u>strapping</u> young man. He eats nutritious food and exercises every day.

strenuous - (adj.) demanding great physical strength or endurance. e.g. - Lifting the heavy box was a very <u>strenuous</u> task. Der. (adv.) strenuously.

strewn - (p. part.) spread; scattered; thrown about. e.g. - His bedroom was a mess. Everything was <u>strewn</u> about. Der. (v.) strew.

strife - (n.) conflict; friction. e.g. - There is a good deal of <u>strife</u> in the government. Politicians are always arguing about differing viewpoints.

stringent - (adj.) strict or rigid. e.g. - Bruce's father has many <u>stringent</u> rules and often punishes him. Der. (adv.) stringently.

strip - (n.) an individual, thin piece of sthg. e.g. - The beef <u>strips</u> were grilled on the barbecue.

strive (for/to) - (v.) to attempt sthg with serious energy and effort. He is an excellent student and <u>strives</u> for perfection in all his homework assignments.

structure - (n.) a building. e.g. - The city has various <u>structures</u>, including office buildings, apartment buildings, and single-family homes. Der. (v.) structure; (adj.) structural.

studious - (adj.) relating to individuals who read or study extensively. e.g. - Shanti is very <u>studious</u>. She spends five hours a day doing her homework.

stuffy - (adj.) inflexible in following tradition or custom. e.g. - He is so <u>stuffy</u> that most people think he is inflexible and boring. Der. (n.) stuffiness; (adv.) stuffily.

stumbling block - (id.) something that prevents or hinders progress. (syn.) hindrance, obstacle, barrier. e.g. - His poor health was a <u>stumbling block</u> towards his performance at work.

stupendous - (adj.) amazing or astounding in size. e.g. - The circus was <u>stupendous</u>. It included one hundred different kinds of animals. Der. (adv.) stupendously.

sturdy - (adj.) relating to objects that are strong and solid. e.g. - This table is <u>sturdy</u> and can hold quite heavy objects. Der. (adv.) sturdily.

sty - (n.) a small house for a pig. e.g. - The pig was sleeping in its <u>sty</u> in order to be protected from the sunlight.

subdued - (adj.) to control or reduce in degree of feeling. e.g. - Hana was quite angry earlier in the week, but she's feeling more <u>subdued</u> now.

subject (to) - (v.) to force to experience or endure something, esp. something unpleasant or unwanted. e.g. - He was <u>subjected</u> to punishment from his father for arriving home late.

subjugate - (v.) to suppress or take control of. e.g. - The police attempted to subjugate the rioters. Der. (n.) subjugation.

submerge - (v.) to place an object under the surface of the water. e.g. - Katie frightened us when she submerged herself in the lake for three minutes. We were worried that she might have drowned. Der. (n.) submergence.

subordinate - (adj.) being less in rank or authority. e.g. - He has a subordinate position in the company. There are ten managers in authority over him. Der. (n.) subordination, subordinate; (v.) subordinate.

subscribe - (v.) to receive publications or services at regular time intervals in exchange for a fee. e.g. - Adam subscribes to that publication and receives a magazine every month. Der. (n.) subscription; (n.) subscriber.

subsequent - (adj.) following in sequence, order, or time. e.g. - Subsequent to secondary school, he attended university. Der. (adv.) subsequently.

subside - (v.) to settle downwards. e.g. - The ground subsided during the earthquake. Geologists now estimate that it is three inches lower than before. Der. (n.) subsidence.

subsistence - (n.) the minimum amount of food necessary for human existence. e.g. - Children in certain countries in Africa do not have enough food for normal subsistence. Some of them are starving. Der. (v.) subsist.

subterfuge - (n.) trickery used in order free oneself from blame or responsibility. e.g. - The suspect's subterfuge consisted of telling the police that his identical twin brother had committed the crime.

sumptuous - (adj.) extremely rich in texture or quality. e.g. – Buckingham Palace has sumptuous decorations. Der. (n.) sumptuousness; (adv.) sumptuously.

supercilious - (adj.) arrogant; conceited. e.g. - He is the most supercilious person I know. He thinks he knows everything about everything. Der. (n.) superciliousness; (adv.) superciliously.

superficial - (adj.) not deep or profound; surface. e.g. - Debra is a superficial woman. Her only interests are clothes and make-up. Der. (adv.) superficially.

superfluous - (adj.) beyond what is necessary. e.g. - The teacher asked for a 300 word composition. Writing 1,000 words was totally superfluous. Der. (n.) superfluity; (adv.) superfluously.

supersede - (v.) to cause to become outdated as a result of being replaced. e.g. - That law is no longer effective as it has been superseded by a new law. Der. (n.) supersession.

superstition - (n.) a belief in supernatural powers or occurrences. e.g. - She believed in the superstition that black cats cause bad luck. Der. (adj.) superstitious; (adv.) superstitiously.

suppress - (v.) to cause to stop or prevent for a period of time. e.g. - This syrup will suppress your cough for three hours. Der. (n.) suppression, suppressant; (adj.) suppressed.

surge - (v.) to rise or move forward suddenly. e.g. - The fans, who had been waiting for hours, <u>surged</u> into the stadium when the gates were finally opened. Der. (n.) surge.

surplus - (n.) an excessive quantity, beyond what is required or necessary. e.g. - The army had a <u>surplus</u> of boots, which were stored in a warehouse.

suspect - (n.) an individual who has committed a crime. e.g. - He is a <u>suspect</u> in the crime since his fingerprints were found at the crime scene. Der. (v.) suspect.

sustenance - (n.) food; nourishment. e.g. - Healthy food and clean water are necessary for human <u>sustenance</u>. Der. (v.) sustain.

sweet tooth - (id.) to enjoy eating sweets very much. e.g. - He has a <u>sweet tooth</u> and enjoys eating cake and candy.

swelling - (n.) the increase in size of a bodily part as if filled by water. e.g. - The doctor recommended that we put ice on Timothy's twisted ankle to prevent <u>swelling</u>. Der. (v.) swell; (adj.) swollen.

swindler - (n.) an individual who acquires money through fraud or dishonesty. e.g. - Emma lost her life savings to a <u>swindler</u> who promised to invest her money, but later left town with all of it. Der. (v.) swindle.

Exercises – S

Instructions: Complete the sentences below, using one of the words beginning with the letter "S" from the previous section. Note that some gaps require a single word, while others may need a phrasal verb or idiomatic expression. You may also need to change the form of the word. The answers are provided at the end of book.

1) This meal is _____. It is truly delicious.

2) Because of _____ funding, the volunteer centre had to be closed.

3) That water is _____. It is not fit to drink and is beginning to smell bad.

4) My accident caused a _____ to my studies, and I graduated a semester later.

5) You will appear _____ if you never clean your shoes or comb your hair.

6) It is going to be impossible to change her point of view. She always _____.

7) The anti-gravity capsule attempts to _____ flight in outer space.

8) Carrying 120 kilos of luggage through three airports was certainly a _____ task.

9) The political party leader is so _____. He is really corrupt, but he always talks about the importance of being honest.

10) The sales person was actually a _____ who promised to deliver the merchandise, but just took all the money instead.

Words – T

Instructions: Study the words below, paying attention to their meanings as well as how they are used in the example sentences. Then complete the exercise that follows.

tackle - (v.) to attempt with difficulty. e.g. - She put off doing her homework all weekend and finally <u>tackled</u> it on Sunday evening.

take its/their toll - (id.) to begin to affect, esp. negatively. e.g. - Missing several nights of sleep finally <u>took its toll</u> on him.

tale - (n.) a story, esp. one that is not based on the truth. e.g. - He told a tall <u>tale</u> which no one believed.

talk a mile a minute - (id.) to talk very quickly. e.g. - It is so difficult to understand him. He <u>talks a mile a minute</u>.

tangible - (adj.) being perceived by the senses; real; material. e.g. - The insensitive man valued his <u>tangible</u> possessions more than love or friendship. Der. (n.) tangibility; (adv.) tangibly.

tantamount (to) - (adj.) equal to in terms of results or consequences. e.g. - Refusing to tell the entire truth is <u>tantamount</u> to lying.

tap - (v.) to place small listening devices secretly on telephone lines. e.g. - The drug dealer made arrangements with his supplier only over public telephones since he suspected that his private telephone line had been <u>tapped</u>. Der. (n.) tap.

tardiness - (n.) lateness for school or work. e.g. - Jeff's <u>tardiness</u> at work has become a serious problem. He was warned that he will be fired the next time he's late. Der. (adj.) tardy.

tee-totalling - (adj.) totally refraining from the consumption of alcoholic drinks. e.g. - Todd used to be an alcoholic, but now he is <u>tee-totalling</u> and never drinks. Der. (v.) teetotal.

tedious - (adj.) monotonous or tiring. e.g. - Working in a factory assembly line is <u>tedious</u> work. Most factory workers suffer from boredom. Der. (n.) tedium; (adv.) tediously.

temperamental - (adj.) excessively sensitive or unpredictable in mood or state of mind. e.g. - Nathan is so <u>temperamental</u> that you never know what kind of mood he will be in. Der. (n.) temperament; (adv.) temperamentally.

temporal - (adj.) relating to sensual or earthly desires. e.g. - Monks are required to place little importance on <u>temporal</u> needs, such as food and clothing, in order to concentrate on spiritual concerns. Der. (n.) temporality; (adv.) temporally.

tenet - (n.) belief; doctrine; dogma. e.g. - One of the basic <u>tenets</u> of mathematics is that any unknown quantity can be calculated by using the proper equation.

terse - (adj.) unnecessarily brief or abrupt in speech. e.g. - Mia was so <u>terse</u> this morning. When I asked her how she was, she told me that is was none of my business. Der. (n.) terseness; (adv.) tersely.

testament - (n.) written proof relating to the disposal of property after an individual's death. e.g. - An individual's last will and <u>testament</u> is often read after the funeral in order to determine how property should be distributed.

testify - (v.) to make a statement in court under oath. e.g. - Brittney witnessed the bank robbery and must <u>testify</u> in court about what she saw take place. Der. (n.) testimony; (n.) testimonial.

texture - (n.) the quality of the surface or structure of something. The <u>texture</u> of the blanket was soft and fuzzy. Der. (v.) texturize.

That takes the biscuit! - (id.) that is shocking or unbelievable. e.g. - He asked to borrow money from you again. <u>That really takes the biscuit</u>!

thaw - (v.) to return a frozen object to its normal temperature. e.g. - The frozen meat needs to be removed from the freezer and <u>thawed</u> before it can be cooked. Der. (adj.) thawed.

throng - (n.) a crowd or large gathering of people. e.g. - A noisy <u>throng</u> of 100,000 spectators was present at the championship match. Der. (v.) throng.

thwart - (v.) to oppose, prevent, hinder, or frustrate. e.g. - His poor health <u>thwarted</u> his progress in school.

tilt - (v.) to move or lean towards one side. e.g. - The repairman <u>tilted</u> the machine to one side in order to fix it. Der. (n.) tilt; (adj.) tilted.

timid - (adj.) shy; easily embarrassed. e.g. - Parveen is so <u>timid</u> that she is afraid to speak. Der. (n.) timidity; (adv.) timidly.

tiny - (adj.) very small; (syn.) dinky, puny. e.g. - The bug was so <u>tiny</u> that it could hardly be seen.

tipsy - (adj.) dizzy or euphoric, esp. from drunkenness. She felt <u>tipsy</u> after having drunk the bottle of wine. Der. (n.) tipsiness; (adv.) tipsily.

toe the line - (id.) to conform to a rigid standard of behaviour. e.g. - If you want to lose ten pounds in two weeks, you will have to <u>toe the line</u>.

token - (n.) an indication or display of appreciation. e.g. - Please accept this gift as a <u>token</u> of my appreciation for all the help you've given me.

tolerate - (v.) to possess the ability to accept or endure another person's behaviour, esp. when it is offensive or undesirable. e.g. - I don't really enjoy his company, but I can <u>tolerate</u> him sometimes.

topple - (v.) to cause to fall down. e.g. - Many buildings <u>toppled</u> to the ground during the earthquake.

touchy - (id.) overly sensitive or moody. e.g. - She is <u>touchy</u> and hates being criticised.

trail - (n.) a small dirt road that is formed by the movement of traffic or people. e.g. - The hikers walked along the trail through the woods. Der. (v.) trail.

transplant - (n.) the replacement of a bodily organ with another organ from a deceased person. e.g. - The patient's diseased liver was replaced during the transplant operation. Der. (v.) transplant.

treacherous - (adj.) dangerous; (syn.) precarious. e.g. - The weather is treacherous today. Travel is not advised. Der. (n.) treacherousness, treachery; (adv.) treacherously.

treason - (n.) the action of disloyalty or betrayal towards an individual's government of nationality or citizenship. e.g. - The politician was accused of treason for revealing military secrets.

treaty - (n.) an agreement made between or among two or more nations. e.g. - An import/export treaty exists between the U.S. and Japan.

trench - (n.) a long, narrow area that has been dug in the ground; ditch. e.g. - During World War I, soldiers often fought while standing in trenches for protection. Der. (v.) entrench.

trend - (n.) the current preference displayed by the public; tendency. e.g. - Current economic trends show increased activity in the marketplace. Der. (adj.) trendy.

tributary - (n.) a river which enters a larger river or lake. e.g. - The River Ash is a tributary of the River Thames as it flows into the Thames at Lower Sunbury.

trim - (v.) to cut at the edges. e.g. - Hong had her hair trimmed by the hairdresser. She had only an inch cut off. Der. (n.) trim.

troop - (n.) a unit of soldiers in the armed services. e.g. - The troop of soldiers set up camp for the evening.

trunk - (n.) the central wooden part of a tree from which branches grow. e.g. - A tree will fall down if it is cut through the trunk.

trying - (adj.) physically, mentally, or psychologically demanding; (syn.) arduous; enervating. e.g. - Aiko finds her boss's complaints and demands very trying.

turbulent - (adj.) causing the development of violence or disturbance. e.g. - The turbulent atmosphere in the city is a result of disharmony among various races. Der. (n.) turbulence.

turn on a dime - (id.) to have great flexibility in motion. e.g. - This car is one of the finest machines I have ever driven. It can turn on a dime.

turn over a new leaf - (id.) to improve one's behaviour; to change for the better. e.g. - The student promised to turn over a new leaf and start handing in his homework on time.

twig - (n.) a small piece on the branch of a tree. e.g. - Several small twigs were gathered from the forest to start the campfire.

Exercises – T

Instructions: Complete the sentences below, using one of the words beginning with the letter "T" from the previous section. Note that some gaps require a single word, while others may need a phrasal verb or idiomatic expression. You may also need to change the form of the word. The answers are provided at the end of book.

1) You have to _____ in court if you see a crime take place.

2) Her job is difficult and _____. She has thought about quitting many times.

3) We finally _____ the unpleasant task last weekend.

4) The child promised _____ and start behaving better.

5) Saying that you aren't that fond of her is _____ to saying that you really don't like her.

6) His house and car were the _____ indications of his success in life.

7) _____ for class will not be tolerated. Students will have to report to the principal if they are late to class.

8) Artists can be _____ and sensitive to criticism about their work.

9) The _____ of her skin was smooth and silky.

10) A loud _____ of one thousand people started the protest.

Words – U to V

Instructions: Study the words below, paying attention to their meanings as well as how they are used in the example sentences. Then complete the exercise that follows.

ultimatum - (n.) the action of being presented with two difficult or undesirable choices. e.g. - The student received the <u>ultimatum</u> that he would be expelled if his grades did not improve.

unanimous - (adj.) relating to full and total agreement by all members of a group. e.g. - The new law received the <u>unanimous</u> support of all Members of Parliament. Der. (n.) unanimity; (adv.) unanimously.

unconventional - (adj.) non-traditional; very unusual or eccentric. e.g. - Monica is a very <u>unconventional</u> woman. She has many unusual habits. Der. (adv.) unconventionally.

undaunted - (adj.) courageous; not afraid or discouraged by opposition or adversity. e.g. - The soldier was <u>undaunted</u> in spite of the danger he faced in battle. Der. (v.) daunt.

undemonstrative - (adj.) not displaying feeling or emotion. e.g. - Mark is so <u>undemonstrative</u> that we couldn't tell whether he was happy or not. Der. (adv.) undemonstratively.

under the weather - (id.) to feel sick or generally unwell. e.g. - He feels <u>under the weather</u> and has been in bed for four days.

underdeveloped - (adj.) inadequate in terms of preparation, growth, or strength. e.g. My brother is so <u>underdeveloped</u> for his age that he is almost a foot shorter than the other boys in his class. Der. (n.) underdevelopment; (ant.) developed.

undermine - (v.) to weaken gradually. e.g. - His health was <u>undermined</u> by the progression of the disease. Der. (adj.) undermined.

undertaking - (n.) a project, enterprise, or job, especially one of significant size or effort. e.g. - Painting a fifteen-room house in a day was a huge <u>undertaking</u>. Der. (n.) undertake.

undoing - (n.) ruin; destruction; demise. e.g. - Drug abuse was his <u>undoing</u>. He lost his family, his job, and his home.

uniformity - (n.) similarity in size, shape, weight, or quality. e.g. - The factory strives for <u>uniformity</u> in quality of all the goods it manufactures. Der. (adv.) uniform. Der. (adv.) uniformly.

unsavoury - (adj.) distasteful; (syn.) insipid. e.g. - This soup is <u>unsavoury</u> and isn't fit to eat. Der. (ant.) savoury.

unscrupulous - (adj.) without honest or integrity. e.g. - She lost all her money in an <u>unscrupulous</u> business arrangement. Der. (n.) unscrupulousness; (adv.) unscrupulously.

unwavering - (adj.) constant; unchanging. e.g. - He had always been a football fanatic. His enthusiasm for the sport is <u>unwavering</u>.

up to doing sthg - (id.) to be in the mood to do something. e.g. - I'm not <u>up to</u> going out tonight. Let's stay home.

upheaval - (n.) the action of causing disturbance or disorder. e.g. - He always causes <u>upheaval</u> in the class with his constant interruptions. Der. (v.) upheave.

utmost - (adj.) the highest or greatest aspect of something. e.g. - Brushing your teeth daily is of the <u>utmost</u> importance for good dental hygiene.

vacillate - (v.) to waver back and forth between alternative choices. e.g. - She continued to <u>vacillate</u> between the two choices and was unable to make a decision. Der. (n.) vacillation; (adj.) vacillated, vacillating; (adv.) vacillatingly.

valiantly - (adv.) being done with strength, bravery, and determination; heroically. e.g. - The fireman died <u>valiantly</u> in the blaze, saving the life of a small child. Der. (adj.) valiant.

variation - (n.) change or alteration. e.g. – My father does not like change. He gets upset if there is any <u>variation</u> in his normal daily routine. Der. (n.) variance; (v.) vary; (adj.) varied.

vault - (1)(n.) a burial chamber; (2)(n.) a place used for storing valuables. e.g. - (1) The bodies of murder victims are often stored in <u>vaults</u> which may be re-opened in the event that further examinations are necessary. (2) The millionaire stored his money and other valuables in a <u>vault</u>.

ventilation - (n.) the action of receiving sufficient air or oxygen. e.g.- The window was opened so that the room could receive some <u>ventilation</u>. Der. (v.) ventilate; (adj.) ventilated.

venture - (n.) a business arrangement involving risk or speculation. e.g. - Gambling at Las Vegas can be a dangerous <u>venture</u>.

venue - (n.) the place or location at which an event takes place. e.g. - The stadium is the <u>venue</u> for the concert.

verdict - (n.) decision by a jury in court. e.g. - If the jury returns a <u>verdict</u> of guilty at the end of a trial, the suspect will be sent to prison.

verify - (v.) to determine the truth of. e.g. - A lie detector test is often used to <u>verify</u> the details of statements given by suspects. Der. (n.) verification, verity; veracity (adj.) verified.

versatile - (adj.) possessing many skills, talents, or uses. e.g. - My niece is a very <u>versatile</u> musician. She knows how to play the piano and guitar and can also sing beautifully. Der. (n.) versatility.

vessel - (n.) a ship or boat. e.g. - He owns an expensive yacht. It is really an amazing <u>vessel</u> and has the most modern equipment.

vicious - (adj.) relating to the desire to cause harm or injury; cruel. e.g. - The lies you said about my mother were <u>vicious</u>. You only wanted to hurt me. Der. (n.) viciousness; (adv.) viciously.

vicissitude - (n.) a change in a situation or circumstance, generally for the worse. e.g. - There have been many <u>vicissitudes</u> in the economy this year, including a rise in unemployment and an increase in the rate of inflation. Der. (n.) vicissitudinous.

victuals - (n.) food. e.g. - Our <u>victuals</u> are stored in the refrigerator and kitchen cupboards.

vie - (v.) to engage in competition or rivalry. e.g. - The two teams will <u>vie</u> for the championship on Sunday.

vigilant - exercising extreme care or caution in outlook. e.g. - The doctors were <u>vigilant</u> in watching the president after his heart attack. Der. (n.) vigilance; (adv.) vigilantly.

villain - (n.) dishonest person; criminal; crook. e.g. - The <u>villain</u> cheated the elderly couple out of their life savings. Der. (v.) vilify.

vindication - (n.) the action of seeking revenge or setting free from blame. e.g. - His <u>vindication</u> from the charge of murder came when the judge announced that he was not guilty. Der. (v.) vindicate.

violation - (n.) offense; crime. e.g. - It is a <u>violation</u> of traffic laws to drive a car after dark without turning its lights on. Der. (v.) violate.

virile - (adj.) the quality of being full of strength and energy. e.g. - The <u>virile</u> weight-lifter managed to lift seven hundred pounds.

vital - (adj.) very important or necessary. e.g. - Studying is <u>vital</u> if you want to do well on your final examinations. Der. (adv.) vitally.

vocational - (adj.) relating to training or education in a particular skill or craft. e.g. - The college offers many <u>vocational</u> courses, including woodworking and automotive repair. Der. (n.) vocation.

voluble - (adj.) very talkative. e.g. - My best friend is so <u>voluble</u> that she is almost always talking.

voluntarily - (adv.) being done by free choice, without external pressure or influence. e.g. - My neighbor works at the local hospital <u>voluntarily</u> three times a week, even though he receives no payment for his services. Der. (n.) volunteer; (v.) volunteer; (adj.) voluntary.

vow - (n.) promise. e.g. - During the marriage ceremony, the groom made a <u>vow</u> to be faithful to his wife until death. Der. (v.) vow.

vulgar - (adj.) offensive in content or expression; lewd; in bad taste. e.g. - Many CDs have warnings because their songs contain <u>vulgar</u> lyrics. Der. (n.) vulgarity.

Exercises – U to V

Instructions: Complete the sentences below, using one of the words beginning with the letters "U" to "V" from the previous section. Note that some gaps require a single word, while others may need a phrasal verb or idiomatic expression. You may also need to change the form of the word. The answers are provided at the end of book.

1) He _____ between two versions of the story, so it was impossible to tell which one was true.

2) The progress of the construction of the building was _____ by the poor weather.

3) If the jury returns a _____ of innocent, the suspect will be released.

4) Adopting a child is an incredible _____. So much responsibility is involved in raising a child.

5) The management of that company is very _____. I have never heard of any other company that permits employees to sleep on the job.

6) The auditorium is the _____ for the graduation ceremony.

7) _____ in the economy have caused many companies to go out of business in recent years.

8) I gave my boyfriend the _____ that I would leave him if he continued to flirt with other women.

9) Her love for her children is _____. Nothing could change her feelings.

10) Using profanity, swearing, and spitting are _____ habits.

Words W to Z

Instructions: Study the words below, paying attention to their meanings as well as how they are used in the example sentences. Then complete the exercise that follows.

wag - (v.) the side-to-side motion made by a dog's tail. e g. - The happy dog stood by the road wagging its tail. Der. (n.) wag.

ward - (n.) an individual under custody or guardianship. a.g. - The orphaned child had no living relatives and became a ward of the state, which provided food and shelter.

warp - (v.) to cause wood to become disfigured as a result of exposure to water or moisture. e.g. - The surface of the table top is not level. The water leaking from the ceiling has warped it. Der. (adj.) warped. Der. (n.) warp.

wary - (adj.) cautious because of concerns or worries about something, especially about safety. e.g. - He was very wary of traveling through such a bad neighbourhood. Der. (n.) wariness; (adv.) warily.

wayward - (adj.) being done contrary to the expectations of society or others. e.g. - Maria was a wayward adolescent. She helped rob a bank when she was just thirteen.

weary - (adj.) very tired. e.g. - The trip lasted thirty-two hours and the travellers were quite weary from the journey. Der. (adv.) wearily.

whim - (n.) a sudden or eccentric idea or impulse. e.g. - She dyed her hair bright purple on a whim. Der. (adj.) whimsical.

whip - (n.) a device consisting of a handle and a long leather strap, used for the purpose of torturing or beating. e.g. - The farmer used the whip to strike the horse in order to move it forward. Der. (v.) whip.

wholesome - (adj.) acceptable in terms of health, character, or morals. e.g. - Milk is a wholesome drink because it is full of vitamins and minerals. Der. (n.) wholesomeness.

widespread - (adj.) existing or extending over a wide area or region; extensive. e.g. - Drug addiction is so widespread that it is now a very serious problem in every American city.

winsome - (adj.) charming; pleasant; cheerful; (syn.) affable, amiable, cordial. e.g. - Jane is a very winsome girl. She is rarely unhappy.

wistful - (adj.) causing sadness or depression. e.g. - Alison felt wistful when her marriage ended, and she went into a deep depression. Der. (adv.) wistfully.

wither - (v.) to lack freshness as a result of becoming dried out. e.g. - If you don't put those flowers in some water, they will wither. Der. (adj.) withered.

witness - (n.) an individual who saw a crime being committed. e.g. - Yuki was a witness to the car accident. She saw it happen when she was standing across the street. Der. (v.) witness.

87

© COPYRIGHT 1995-2018. Exam SAM Study Aids & Media dba www.examsam.com
This material may not be copied or reproduced in any form.

witty - (adj.) amusing and intelligent. e.g. - Mohammed told a <u>witty</u> joke which made us all laugh. Der. (n.) wit; (adv.) wittily.

wrath - (n.) anger. e.g. - You will suffer the <u>wrath</u> of your parents if you disobey them.

wretched - (adj.) being particularly bad in quality; (syn.) dismal. e.g. - The team's performance was <u>wretched</u> and, of course, they lost the game. Der. (n.) wretchedness; (adv.) wretchedly.

yank - (v.) to pull suddenly and forcefully. e.g. - The door was stuck and we had to <u>yank</u> it in order to open it.

yearn - (v.) to crave or desire. e.g. - Having grown tired of city life, William <u>yearned</u> for a life in the country. Der. (n.) yearning.

you can count on it - (id.) you can depend on it; it is certain to happen. e.g. - <u>You can count on</u> her coming to the party. She promised to be there.

zealot - (n.) an individual displaying unreasonable enthusiasm; fanatic. e.g. - Susan is an absolute <u>zealot</u> about her exercise routine. She goes to the gym twice a day. Der. (adj.) zealous; (adv.) zealously.

Exercises – W to Z

Instructions: Complete the sentences below, using one of the words beginning with the letters "W" to "Z" from the previous section. Note that some gaps require a single word, while others may need a phrasal verb or idiomatic expression. You may also need to change the form of the word. The answers are provided at the end of book.

1) He was _____ of beginning the journey when it was raining so heavily.

2) She is a _____ about keeping the house clean. She cleans it every day.

3) These fresh herbs will _____ if it is too hot in the kitchen.

4) I felt absolutely _____ yesterday. I couldn't even get out of bed

5) He couldn't take care of himself because of his health and financial problems, and he finally had to become a _____ of the state

6) She _____ the accident and had to tell the police officer what she had seen.

7) She is such a _____ person. She tells such funny jokes.

8) Having been away from home for a year, Yoko _____ to see her family.

9) She was so _____ when she moved and had to say goodbye to all her good friends.

10) Those who fail to follow social norms will suffer the _____ of society.

Answers – A:

1) affiliation

2) accompany

3) animosity

4) arduous

5) accessible

6) adhesive

7) adversaries

8) alibi

9) alluded

10) ambiance

Answers – B:

1) beating around the bush

2) butter

3) breach

4) buoys

5) broke down

6) bland

7) belittles

8) baffled

9) blandishment

10) bored to tears

Answers – D:

1) chortled

2) capsized

3) cavity

4) clutter

5) clandestine

6) collaboration

7) classifies

8) capitulated

9) charming

10) cogent

Answers – D:

1) dense

2) despicable

3) diligent

4) dismantled

5) diversified

6) downfall

7) dysfunction

8) dingy

9) desperation

10) defect

Answers – E:

1) elusive

2) enervating

3) enterprises

4) exacerbate

5) extenuating

6) entails

7) effigy

8) eerie

9) embezzling

10) endeavour

Answers – F:

1) facetious

2) flanked

3) fortuitous

4) frivolous

5) fundamental

6) fulsome

7) flourish

8) foiled

9) frolicking

10) fizzle out

Answers – G to H:

1) get in touch

2) garnishes

3) handy

4) grumbles

5) grasping at straws

6) hoarse

7) hit the spot

8) hunch

9) garbled

10) hushed

Answers – I:

1) immaculate

2) implicated or incriminated

3) in the red

4) inhabitant

5) impeccable

6) instigated

7) idle

8) implored

9) indefatigable

10) impact

Answers – J to L:

1) jotted down

2) latent

3) loquacious

4) knack

5) jumble

6) label

7) luxurious

8) liabilities

9) licentious

10) jurisdiction

Answers – M to O:

1) obliterated

2) nominated

3) obstinate

4) overabundance

5) nit-picks

6) magnanimity

7) noxious

8) mandatory

9) ostentatious

10) mitigated

Answers – P:

1) phlegmatic

2) pillaged

3) peak

4) pioneer

5) precarious or prostrate

6) putrid

7) playing with fire

8) protracted

9) perceptible

10) pull through

Answers – Q to R:

1) rehabilitation

2) render

3) quaint

4) recuperate

5) quest

6) relinquish

7) recruitment

8) quirk

9) retrospect

10) reluctant

Answers – S:

1) scrumptious

2) scant

3) stagnant

4) setback

5) slovenly

6) sticks to her guns

7) simulate

8) strenuous

9) sanctimonious

10) swindler

Answers – T:

1) testify

2) trying or tedious

3) tackled

4) to turn over a new leaf

5) tantamount

6) tangible

7) tardiness

8) touchy

9) texture

10) throng

Answers – U to V:

1) vacillated

2) undermined

3) verdict

4) undertaking

5) unconventional

6) venue

7) vicissitudes

8) ultimatum

9) unwavering

10) vulgar

Answers – W to Z:

1) wary

2) zealot

3) wither

4) wretched

5) ward

6) witnessed

7) witty

8) yearned

9) wistful

10) wrath

Manufactured by Amazon.ca
Bolton, ON